The Kansas Blue Sky Act of 1911

David Ress

The Kansas Blue Sky Act of 1911

An Experiment in Securities Regulation and its Impact

palgrave
macmillan

David Ress
School of Humanities
University of New England
Armidale, NSW, Australia

ISBN 978-3-031-43830-1 ISBN 978-3-031-43831-8 (eBook)
https://doi.org/10.1007/978-3-031-43831-8

This Palgrave Macmillan imprint is published by the registered company Springer Nature Switzerland AG
The registered company address is: Gewerbestrasse 11, 6330 Cham, Switzerland

Paper in this product is recyclable.

To Andy Obermueller, for many years of friendship, for wisdom shared on finance and on life, and for so many tales of his home state, since, as Vachel Lindsey wrote:

For all men dream in Kansas,
By noonday and by night,
By sunrise yellow, red and wild,
And moonrise wild and white

Preface: Blue Sky and Buyer Beware

Turning off Kansas Route 18 into Lincoln Center, you pass a stately courthouse, made of the beige limestone "post rock" that people here in central Kansas used as fence posts, since trees are pretty scarce on these dry shortgrass plains. Kitty-corner, there's the old bank building, another limestone stalwart: the forty-some commercial buildings in the next three blocks are humbler brick or metal, some are empty. In little towns like this, back when it was more of a project to travel the 42 miles to Salina or even farther to Wichita or Topeka, commerce here pretty much happened on those three blocks of Lincoln Avenue, and people here dealt with neighbors, the same neighbors they'd dealt with for years and expected to continue dealing with for many years to come: *caveat emptor*, the legal doctrine of buyer beware necessarily seemed less certain here. Wondering about why it was Kansas that pioneered the regulation of sales of stock and bonds with its Blue Sky Act of 1911, and hearing tales of the old days in places like Lincoln Center, it struck me that the explanation was precisely the distinctive nature of commerce in an isolated, miniature economy of places like Lincoln Center -- a better explanation, in fact, that the usual quick guess that the kind of securities regulation in state "blue sky acts" was simply a failed excess of the Progressive Era.

In part, I wanted to ask about the roots of blue sky law because, as a journalist in Virginia, I had seen that the blue sky approach was not necessarily a failure. I had seen, as well, reporting on capital markets in Canada, Britain, and the United States that the alternative, typified in the much more easygoing approach of the U.S. Securities Act of 1933 and Securities Exchange Act of 1934, along with the refinements to federal securities law that followed, had not prevented many decades of offerings that simply should not have been made. In some cases, they were outright frauds, in others, they represented a shifting of risk from the organizers of a speculative venture to the public that was simply unfair. The cases of Enron, or Tyco—or earlier, the postwar Kaiser-Frazer or Tucker Motors deals, like the uranium boom of the 1950s or penny stock deals from the 1960s on—suggested to me that federal law could not do what blue sky law could.

The story of the Blue Sky Act, I found, is a story of an America that's not really there any more, rather like those empty storefronts on Lincoln's main street. It's a story, too, about how Americans think about regulation and the way it opposes a belief in liberty with an inclination to accept what could be characterized as paternalism.

I owe thanks to Professor Jennifer Clark, of the University of Adelaide, who sparked my interest in the history of ideas, as well as Professors David Roberts and Matthew Dillon of the University of New England and Kristen Epps at Kansas State University. Ron Thomas, of the Virginia Bureau of Securities, Commissioner Joe Face, of the Virginia Bureau of Financial Institutions and his predecessor, the late Sidney Bailey, along with Commissioner Scott White of the Virginia Bureau of Insurance and his predecessor, the late Al Gross, as well as former deputy commissioner of the New Jersey Department of Banking and Insurance, Peter Hart, were valued guides to the mysteries of financial regulation. Virginia legislators Lee Ware, Terry Kilgore, Chap Petersen, and Thomas K. Norment were ever helpful on the political dynamics of state financial regulation, as was Jay Speer of the Virginia Poverty Law Center and Jean Ann Fox, of the Consumer Federation of America. Lauren Gray, head of reference at the Kansas State Archives, was a patient guide through state records. My friend Andy Obermueller edited many of my reports on explorations of the underworld of penny stocks and boiler rooms. Any errors are, of course, entirely mine.

Armidale, Australia David Ress

Contents

About the Author

David Ress is an honorary research associate at the University of New England (Australia), where he earned his Ph.D. in history. His research focuses on settler societies, land rights, and financial history. A journalist who has reported on capital markets in Canada, Britain, and the United States, he is the author of Governor Coles and the Vote to Forbid Slavery in Illinois; Municipal Accountability in the American Age of Reform; The Half Breed Tracts; and Deeds, Titles, and Changing Concepts of Land Rights.

CHAPTER 1

Paternalism Versus Autonomy in Regulation: The Naïf, the Slicker, and the Busybody

Abstract The first comprehensive effort to regulate the sale of stocks and bonds to the public, the Kansas Blue Sky Act of 1911, substituted the judgment of a state official for the investor's, unlike the regulatory approach adopted with the U.S. Securities Act of 1933. The Act's paternalism was acceptable for a time because it reflected the values and patterns of commerce of small rural communities like the home of the Act's author, Kansas Banking Commissioner Joseph N. Dolley. The stories Dolley told about innocents who were taken in tapped still-important popular belief. But the Kansas model was rejected eventually because the ease of buying and selling shares on stock exchanges and the many tales of easy money to be made through speculation presented Blue Sky Act regulation as a paternalistic overreach of state power.

Keywords Kansas · Securities regulation · Fraud · Blue Sky Act · Securities sales · Paternalism

The slickly dressed stranger who called himself Richard J. Thompkins of the Pan-American Plantations Company had just hopped off his train in a small Kansas town and, as was his wont, picked up a copy of the local weekly newspaper to scan the obituaries. What caught his eye this time, or so Kansas Bank Commissioner Joseph N. Dolley's tale went, was the item

D. Ress, *The Kansas Blue Sky Act of 1911*,
https://doi.org/10.1007/978-3-031-43831-8_1

reporting the recent death of a railroad machinist. The obituary noted that he had been a member of a fraternal order, one that Thompkins knew was essentially a burial insurance company. It took just a few minutes, leafing through a city directory or chatting to a storekeeper, for Thompkins to get directions to the pretty little cottage where the machinist's widow lived. Hastening there, arriving just after she had finished giving her three little children their lunch and bustled them back off to school for the afternoon, Thompkins caught the widow as she finished dressing up for a trip downtown. She was planning to take the $2,000 life insurance check from her late husband's fraternal society to the local building and loan association to pay off the balance of the mortgage on her home.[1]

In placing Mr. Thompkins at the widow's door as she was about to pay off her mortgage, Commissioner Dolley set the stage for a melodramatic tale that, for a time in the early twentieth century, inspired an early, heavy-handed exercise of state power to look out for people who seemed unable to look for themselves. His approach would briefly sweep aside what had been a fundamental legal rule governing buying and selling—*caveat emptor*, the lawyer's Latin tag for buyer beware—and would spark dire warnings, never realized, that his proposed power to ban some sales of shares would shut down business growth and innovation. Dolley's tales of his various (and mainly fictional) Messrs. Thompkins and Kansan widows made the point he wanted to stress—that men like him needed to intervene to stop otherwise attractive deals—by summoning up some easily-recognized rural American types. There was the trickster, cast as city slicker. There was the naïf, the innocent, in the role of beleaguered widow or bewildered hayseed. In the background, the wise but all-too-often disregarded counselor who, in Dolley's tales, if not his opponents', would never seem to be merely the busybody, so easily dismissed as a comic figure or disrupter of community peace.

They all helped make briefly acceptable what critics from the investment banking and stock-brokering world would call the paternalism of Dolley's Blue Sky Act of 1911. The Act was the first effective effort to regulate securities dealing in the United States, so-called because Mr. Thompkins and his ilk had nothing more real on offer than shares in the big blue Kansas skies. Dolley's tales were effective because they used the folk types of city slicker and country innocent to reinforce conventions about investment that were rooted in the ways people in small, self-contained communities like his own Maple Hill, Kansas, believed business ought to be conducted.

Investment bankers, the firms that arranged sales of company stocks and bonds, meanwhile, had tales of their own to tell as they made their case against Blue Sky laws patterned on Dolley's model. To appeal to a people who still saw themselves as proudly self-sufficient, the bankers' tales called up the sharp-witted operators and bold adventurers who starred in other folk takes, as well as new mythologies about wealth and enterprise. Ultimately, their stories of self-sufficiency reinforced a general shift in political opinion that saw efforts to regulate business behavior—including Blue Sky laws—as a paternalistic infringement on Americans' liberty. Their tales, too, worked because they contained a newer, more attractive idea about investment, and about how shareholding might be a path toward effortless wealth.

Dolley's Blue Sky Act empowered him (and would empower officials in the several states that adopted his model) to step between the trickster and the naïf by simply banning sale of a stock or bond, before the trickster could begin a sales pitch. The legislators who enacted Blue Sky laws, the public that welcomed them and the officials that enforced them did so out of a belief, rarely explicitly acknowledged, that the innocent here, the hayseed, was incompetent to manage his or her own savings. Rarely admitted, too, was this: Dolley believed that only some—and not very many—shares of company stock or corporate bonds were appropriate vehicles for the public's savings, a view founded on his decades as a small hamlet's credit-granting merchant and later banker: the wise counselor, as folk tales might have it. This view would become economic heresy in the years after World War I, and with that the political will to regulate offerings and so protect people's savings faded.

For those in the booming business of selling stock, the stakes in the campaign against Blue Sky laws were high. Dolley's law allowed him to ban inappropriate offerings, everything from claims to unproven oil or mineral reserves to irrigation ventures that could not work to start-up companies whose organizers put up none of their own money. The Blue Sky Act substituted his judgment (and that of his successors as Banking Commissioner and later staff of the Kansas Corporation Commission) for any other Kansans' good sense. My aim here is to ask why what could be so easily criticized as the extreme paternalism of Blue Sky law could nevertheless be so easily accepted, and then in the 1920s boom years so easily shed. The history of how Blue Sky laws arose and were superseded is a story of popular views about individuals' freedom to choose their own courses as opposed to what society might do to protect them from making bad choices; an ever-shifting balance of opinions that still drives American politics. It is also a story about popular understanding of what, exactly, investing—as distinct from saving—really means, as well as what financial risks and market speculation really entail.

The Kansas Blue Sky Act, then, was rooted in a belief—never made explicit yet essential to its justification—that most Kansans were unable to decide for themselves about how to direct their savings. It assumed that Dolley and state government officials like him knew better than anyone else how best to look after any individual's financial interests. The Blue Sky Act reached, proactively, after more transactions than the outright frauds that were the only (if generally ineffective) way in American (and Anglo-American) law to trump the *caveat emptor*—buyer beware—rule of law.[2] It could do so because Dolley, like most people in tiny self-contained communities like Maple Hill, Kansas, where he had long made a living as a grocer and banker, did not believe in the *caveat emptor* rule's rigid view that buyers should have no recourse if they were victims of their own folly. It was a way of doing business that was unsustainable in Maple Hill and places like that little Wabaunsee County hamlet, for when people deal with neighbors in such a tiny place, neighbors with whom they will have to deal for many years to come, *caveat emptor* undermines the trust necessary for this mode of commerce. Trust abused is what the tale of Mr. Thompkins and Widow is about; trust, too, is what made the daily commerce in cash-short farm communities possible. Kansas judges were, not surprisingly, more skeptical about *caveat emptor* than were their counterparts in more urban centers.[3]

Even by the first decades of the twentieth century, Maple Hill, like the unnamed (and possibly fictitious) Kansan whistle-stop where Mr. Thompkins and the widow played out their small morality tale, was no longer really like the communities in which most Americans lived, though little rural hamlets like Maple Hill were still very much part of the stories Americans told themselves about themselves. Inspired by Dolley's tales of abuse and Kansas's success in reining in the various Mr. Thompkins working the countryside, almost a dozen other states quickly enacted their own strict Blue Sky laws, modeled on the Kansas law. Dolley had launched a movement. But a fierce counterattack by a new-formed association of investment bankers, along with thrilling tales of easy gains thanks to the interwar stock market boom, made a successful case that Dolley's idea was either a simple overreach of a Progressive Era impulse of paternalism—much like Prohibition, that other irritating product of small-town busybodies like the saloon-wrecking Kansan Carrie Nation—or a greedy impulse of a banker to keep hold of his depositors' funds. Opponents alleged Blue Sky laws did not work; indeed, could not work. Their arguments, framed within popularized versions of contemporary economic analysis, eventually appealed to a changing Americana public, a more urban and less financially pressed public, than did the simple, folk-style tales Dolley retailed.

It has not been to tales like the ones Dolley told that the historiography of paternalism in politics and government has turned. Nor do Dolley's tales, or those proffered by his opponents, figure in the ways the handful of passing discussions of the Blue Sky laws themselves, or in histories of the evolution of securities and stock market regulation.[4] The limited historiography of securities regulation sees the Blue Sky law movement as a fairly minor Progressive Era reform and example of that movement's paternalistic impulse; to be precise, of what from the view of many scholars of economic and financial history and theory looks like excessive paternalism.[5] Yet Blue Sky regulation, in fact, was of little interest to the Progressive Party, to Wilsonian Democrats, or to the Progressive wing of the Republican Party; Theodore Roosevelt and Woodrow Wilson would both say they did not believe in interfering with what people did with their savings. While historians paint the rise of paternalism in the Progressive Era as the product of a newly well-off urban middle class, urban phenomenon, and the retreat from paternalism as the result of the concerted efforts of a handful of business leaders reacting to the New Deal, Blue Sky law paternalism in contrast was a phenomenon of a disappearing rural world for which many Americans were quite nostalgic.[6]

Echoing Dolley's contemporary opponents' arguments that Blue Sky laws shut the door on legitimate investments and were an overreaction to an over-hyped problem of fraud, other analyses paint the retreat from Blue Sky law paternalism as a dawning understanding of the logic of free markets. Macro-level political and economic processes were, in this view, the drivers of the balances struck between paternalism and liberty. Dolley, in these analyses, was a mere tool of a lobby of small banks and an early "regulatory entrepreneur"—that is, someone building a career by manipulating government policy.[7] These macro-level analyses, however, rely almost entirely on the narrow foundation of a study of Dolley's actions over the first year of the Blue Sky Act's operation by Canadian Undersecretary of State Thomas Mulvey, a lawyer whose textbook *Dominion Company Law* would become a basic guide to Canadian corporate law, as well as on complaints from investment bankers of aggressive but inconsistent decisions that blocked many suitable, conservative investments but that sometimes allowed fraudulent ones.[8] Kansas records, along with those of other early Blue Sky states, belie these views, as Chapter 4 will show. Moreover, in those states, as in Kansas, Dolley's model of securities regulation reined in sales of fraudulent securities and of the securities offerings that were his real target—the inappropriately speculative. Individuals' savings were protected, as Dolley intended, and to a degree more significant than either investment bankers, the authors of the federal Securities Act of 1933 or later histories would admit.

What both the Progressive movement and Blue Sky Act critics miss, moreover, is that Dolley found a way to balance paternalism and liberty. He found it in a vanishing pattern of American community norms: the self-contained mini-economies and societies of the rural mid-continent. The kind of stories Dolley told, like the stories Americans told themselves about this way of life that fewer and fewer actually experienced, were compelling at a time of rapid growth of cities and brutally efficient industrial enterprise. These stories, like Blue Sky Act itself, expressed a distinctively American philosophy of politics and conception of community life. These stories, too, challenged one important element of other stories Americans like to tell themselves about who they were: the sharp-witted wheeler-dealer, that independent-minded heir of Jefferson's yeoman farmers, able to look out for him- or herself. Dolley did so with his tales of the city slicker, stock boomer, and the country innocent. He faltered, in the end, in the face of newer myths about stock markets and by inadvertently invoking another older folk type: the busybody.

The impact of all this storytelling—Dolley's and his investment banker opponents'—was real. Through the 1910s and 1920s, the marketing of big promises, minimal assets, and fuzzy business plans—oil or gold-mining company shares, for instance, sold on the basis of never-proven reserves—focused on residents of states that had not adopted a Kansas model Blue Sky Act. The Kansas approach, on the other hand, implicitly assumed some investments were simply inappropriate vehicles for the public's savings: many oil and mining shares, start-up firms where the founders invested little or nothing of their own money and offerings where sales agents earned double-digit percentage commissions.

Inappropriateness, however, would come to seem a busybody's obsession. A new way of looking at stocks—essentially as vehicles for trading rather than as an ownership share entitling the holder to a continuing stream of dividends—and tales of ever-rising stock markets took hold in the 1920s. It was only after the stock market crash of 1929 that popular pressure for a regulatory crackdown on securities markets eventually prompted federal laws that superseded state regulation. These laws, however, merely required filing and public disclosure of the financial details of an offering. They did not forbid offerings, as Dolley's law had, because the authors of these laws and the legislators who enacted them did not share Dolley's belief that broad classes of securities were inappropriate for a wise public, once sufficiently informed. In a sense, the legend of the bold and sharp-witted American and broad acceptance of the concept that shares of stocks were items to be traded and not held for income had superseded earlier tales, like that of Mr. Thompkins and the widow.

The next chapter, then, introduces the country banker Joseph Dolley and the kind of miniature, self-contained economy where his prescriptions about appropriate and inappropriate investments could seem acceptable and not a paternalist overreach. In Chapter 3, as Mr. Thompkins hops off his train, we will see ideas about commerce and finance from a wider world come to places like Dolley's Maple Hill, along with new things to buy and new possibilities of comfort and well-being.[9]

The Blue Sky Act was pitched as an all-out attack on the outsider flim-flam man's offerings, and while it went further to block truly inappropriate deals from businesses that were not necessarily fraudulent businesses, it did not actually affect all that many offerings, Chapter 4 reports. That critique of the Blue Sky Act, then, is unproven, despite its repeated recycling. Dolley's tales of widowed victims—playing to the contemporary view of the archetypical woman as inherently incompetent, a common theme in financial advice books and articles of the day—focused national attention on his initiative, and he fed that with more tales of success, Chapter 5 notes. This led several states to copy the Kansas model, with state officials making a judgment about whether an offering could deliver investors a fair return and banning it if they felt it would not, as Chapter 6 details. Eleven in all took this approach.[10] In Chapter 7, investment bankers pushed back with arguments that Blue Sky laws amounted to an overreach of paternalism, while succeeding for a time in courts by contending that Kansas model laws in Michigan and Ohio were unconstitutional interferences with interstate commerce, in violation of Article 1 of the Constitution.[11] Yet these challenges to the police power of the state would in turn be rejected by the U.S. Supreme Court.[12]

That police power had effect, as seen in Chapter 8. Nevertheless, legal justification of that power and its exercise came as commonly held notions of what a holding of shares of stock actually represented were at this time undergoing a subtle but profound shift. It was the ability to trade shares, rather than to hold them as a vehicle for sharing in a company's profits, that became the focus of attention. As more companies listed shares on stock exchanges and securities firms' effective marketing of the idea that stocks were a path to wealth as well as a way to express a patriotic commitment to American progress, the public began looking in new places for ideas about what to do with their savings, Chapter 9 reports. It would be the stock market price quotations that newspapers began to publish rather than to the promotional materials for blue sky offerings that beguiled would be investors. Trading shares became an end in and of itself, with volumes far outstripping activity in new share issues. The sharp-witted could, after all, look out for him- or herself, especially if he or she could continue playing the market—until the Crash of 1929, of course. And that is a view, as painful memories of the Crash fade, and the federal Securities Act of 1933 and Securities Exchange Act of 1934 took hold, that continues to this day.

Notes

1. Harry F. Kohr, "Blue Sky Law," *Technical World*, March 1912: 38–39.
2. The classic study of the concept of *caveat emptor* is Walton H. Hamilton, "The Ancient Maxim Caveat Emptor," *The Yale Law Journal*, Vol. 40, No. 8 (June 1931): 1133–1187; Edward J. Balleisen, *Fraud: An American History: From Barnum to Madoff* (Princeton: Princeton University Press, 2007): 43–74; Friedrich Kessler, "The Protection of the Consumer Under Modern Sales Law, Part 1: A Comparative Study," *The Yale Law Journal*, Vol. 74, No. 2 (December 1964): 262–285 and Peter Huber, *Liability, The Legal Revolution and Its Consequences* (New York: Basic Books, 1990): 22–23, 190–191, discuss the tension between the rule and public interest in consumer protection; most research has focused on the application of the concept in real estate transactions.

3. See, e.g., Boam et al. v Cohen et al. 94 Kan. 42 (Kansas Supreme Court, 1915); Bailey et al. v Kelly, 86 Kan 911 (1912, Kansas Supreme Court); Fairbanks, Morse & Co. v Walker, 76 Kan 903 (1907, Kansas Supreme Court). Abmeyer v First National Bank of Horton 76 Kan. 877, 92 P. 1109 (Kansas Supreme Court, 1907) at 1110, 1111.
4. Generally, histories of the reform movements of the first half of the twentieth century focus on federal politics and policy, and most set the action in the nation's cities and with the discourse of high culture, although Elizabeth Sanders, *Roots of Reform: Farmers, Workers, and the American State, 1877–1917* (Chicago: University of Chicago Press, 1999) is an exception with her focus on the economic struggles of rural America. While Richard Hofstadter, *The Age of Reform* (New York: Knopf, 1954) sees myth (the agrarian myth of a nation of yeoman farmers) as energizing the earlier Populist movement, the Progressive movement that Dolley's Blue Sky campaign is often linked to was a product of a new, urban class's aspirations: country folkways here count for little. Michael McGerr, *A Fierce Discontent: The Rise and Fall of the Progressive Movement in America, 1870–1920* (New York: Free Press, 2003) who focuses on how city dwellers' worries about class conflict turned them away from individualist ideals to urge reform for social stability. Jackson Lears, *Rebirth of a Nation: The Remaking of Modern America, 1877–1920* (New York: HarperCollins,2009), sees religious ideas of regeneration directing the nation toward both the economic reforms of the era and imperialist expansion, while Maureen Flanagan, *America Reformed: Progressives and Progressivisms, 1890s–1920s* (New York: Oxford University Press, 2007), stresses social justice movements' interest in new roles for government, and Robert Wiebe, *The Search for Order, 1877–1920* (New York: Hill and Wang, 1967) an impulse for rationalism in government. The period is fertile ground for making presentist political cases: as with Murray Rothbard, *The Progressive Era* (Auburn, AL: Mises Institute, 2017) arguing that the period was all about creating cartels and infringement of liberty.
5. Blue Sky laws are presented as a Progressive innovation in Vincent Carosso, *Investment Banking in America* (Cambridge: Harvard University Press, 1970); Rick A. Fleming, "100 Years of Securities Law: Examining a Foundation Laid in the Kansas Blue Sky,"

Washburn Law Journal, Vol. 50, No. 3 (Spring 2011): 583–610; H. Edward Flentje and Joseph A. Aistrup, *Kansas Politics and Government: The Clash of Political Cultures* (Lincoln, NE, 2010) and Edward J. Balleisen, *Fraud. An American history from Barnum to Madoff* (Princeton: Princeton University Press, 2017).

6. For business reaction to Progressive Era reforms see Kim Philips-Fein, *Invisible Hands: The Businessmen's Crusade Against the New Deal* (New York: W. W. Norton, 2010).
7. Kansas model Blue Sky Acts are dismissed as ineffective anti-fraud measures and excessive interference with self-regulating markets in Jonathan R. Macey & Geoffrey P. Miller, "Origin of the Blue Sky Laws," *Texas Law Review*, Vol. 70 (1991): 348–397 (who also argue for Dolley as the regulatory entrepreneur) and Paul G. Mahoney, "The Origins of the Blue-Sky Laws: A Test of Competing Hypotheses," *The Journal of Law & Economics*, Vol. 46, No. 1 (April 2003): 229–251 (arguing that Blue Sky laws were an effort to protect community banks); Louis Loss and Edward Cowett, *Blue Sky Law* (Boston: Little Brown, 1958); James Mofsky, *Blue Sky Restrictions on New Business Promotions* (New York: Matthew Bender & Co, 1971); Daniel Holt, "Acceptable Risk: Law, Regulation, and the Politics of American Financial Markets, 1878–1930," PhD dissertation, University of Virginia, 2008; Meir Statman, "Regulating Financial Markets: Protecting Us from Ourselves and Others," *Financial Analysts Journal*, Vol. 65, No. 3 (May 2009): 22–31. Kenneth R. Gray et al., *Corporate Scandals. The Many Faces of Corporate Greed* (St. Paul: Paragon House, 2005); and Joel Seligman, *The Transformation of Wall Street: A History of the Securities and Exchange Commission and Modern Corporate Finance* (New York: Aspen, 2003): 44–55.
8. Thomas Mulvey, "Blue Sky Law," *Canadian Law Times*, Vol. 36, No. 1 (January 1916): 39. Warren Hayden, an investment banker from Cleveland, was one of many making the case that the Blue Sky Act barred legitimate investments in Proceedings of the Organization Meeting and of the First Annual Convention of the Investment Bankers' Association of America (Chicago: Investment Bankers Association, 1912): 139.
9. The impact of new distribution, transportation, and communication technologies on Americans' susceptibility to get-rich-quick schemes is discussed in, e.g., Edward J. Balleisen, "The 'Sucker

List' and the Evolution of American Business Fraud," *Social Research: An International Quarterly*, Vol. 85, No. 4 (Winter 2018): 701–702; I. Klaus, *Forging Capitalism: Rogues, Swindlers, Frauds, and the Rise of Modern Finance* (New Haven: Yale University Press, 2014); S. Mihm, *A Nation of Counterfeiters: Capitalists, Con Men, and the Making of the United States* (Cambridge, MA: Harvard University Press, 2007).

10. Act of May 18, 1912, chapter 69, 1912 Ariz. Sess. Laws 338; Arkansas Securities Act, No. 214, 1913 Arkansas Acts 904: Idaho Securities Act, chapter 117, 1913 Idaho Session Laws 454; Act of May 2, 1913, No. 143, 1913 Michigan Public Acts 243; Act of March 13, 1913, chapter 85, 1913 Montana Laws 367; Supervision of Investment Companies, chapter 109, 1913 North Dakota Laws 137; Act of April 28, 1913, 1913 Ohio Laws 743; Act of March 14, 1913, chapter 319, 1913 South Dakota Laws 522; Act of September 27, 1913, chapter 31, 1913 Tennessee Public Acts 500; Act of February 13, 1913, No. 170, 1912 Vermont Laws 196; Act of February 6, 1913, ch. 15, 1913 West Virginia. Acts 114.
11. Alabama and New Orleans Transportation Co. v Doyle, 210 Fed 173 (U.S. District Court, Michigan, 1914); Bracey v. Darst, 218 Fed 482 (U.S. District Court, West Virginia, 1914).
12. Hall v. Geiger-Jones Co., 242 U.S. 539 (U.S. Supreme Court, 1917) Merrick v. N. W. Halsey & Co., 242 U.S. 568 (U.S. Supreme Court, 1917).

Bibliography

Abmeyer v First National Bank of Horton 76 Kan. 877, 92 P. 1109 (Kansas Supreme Court, 1907).

Alabama and New Orleans Transportation Co. v Doyle, 210 Fed 173 (U.S. District Court, Michigan, 1914).

Bailey et al. v Kelly, 86 Kan 911 (1912, Kansas Supreme Court).

Balleisen, Edward. 2007. *Fraud: An American History: From Barnum to Madoff*. Princeton: Princeton University Press.

Boam et al. v Cohen et al. 94 Kan. 42 (Kansas Supreme Court, 1915).

Bracey v. Darst, 218 Fed 482 (U.S. District Court, West Virginia, 1914).

Carosso, Vincent. 1970. *Investment Banking in America*. Cambridge: Harvard University Press.

Fairbanks, Morse & Co. v Walker, 76 Kan 903 (1907, Kansas Supreme Court).

Flanagan, Maureen. 2007. *America Reformed: Progressives and Progressivisms, 1890s–1920s*. New York: Oxford University Press.

Fleming, Rick. 2011. "100 Years of Securities Law: Examining a Foundation Laid in the Kansas Blue Sky," *Washburn Law Journal*, 50: 583–610.

Hall v. Geiger-Jones Co., 242 U.S. 539 (U.S. Supreme Court, 1917).

Hamilton, Walton H. 1931. "The Ancient Maxim Caveat Emptor," *The Yale Law Journal*, 40: 1133–1187.

Holt, Daniel. 2008. "Acceptable Risk: Law, Regulation, and the Politics of American Financial Markets, 1878–1930," PhD dissertation, University of Virginia.

Huber, Peter. 1990. *Liability: The Legal Revolution and Its Consequences*. New York: Basic Books.

Kessler, Friedrich. 1964. "The Protection of the Consumer Under Modern Sales Law, Part 1: A Comparative Study," *The Yale Law Journal*, 74 (December 1964): 262–285.

Kohr, Harry F. 1912. "Blue Sky Law," *Technical World*, March: 38–39.

Loss, Louis & Edward Cowett. 1958. *Blue Sky Law*. Boston: Little Brown.

Macey, Jonathan & Geoffrey P. Miller. 1991. "Origin of the Blue Sky Laws," *Texas Law Review*, 70: 348–397.

Mahoney, Paul. 2003. "The Origins of the Blue-Sky Laws: A Test of Competing Hypotheses," *The Journal of Law & Economics*, 46: 229–251.

Merrick v. N. W. Halsey & Co., 242 U.S. 568 (U.S. Supreme Court, 1917).

Mofsky, James. 1971. *Blue Sky Restrictions on New Business Promotions*. New York: Matthew Bender.

Seligman, Joel. 2003. *The Transformation of Wall Street: A History of the Securities and Exchange Commission and Modern Corporate Finance*. New York: Aspen.

Statman, Meir. 2009. "Regulating Financial Markets: Protecting Us from Ourselves and Others," *Financial Analysts Journal*, 65-3: 22–31.

CHAPTER 2

Rural Markets: A Country Banker and a Vanishing Way of Doing Business

Abstract After Kansas Banking Commissioner Joseph Dolley's youth as a sailor carrying cargo for Boston merchants, he became a participant in an entirely way of commerce: the tiny, isolated economy of a rural Kansas hamlet. There, as a grocer and then a banker, he developed a theory of finance that he would later adopt in implementing the Blue Sky Act of 1911.

Keywords Kansas Banking Commissioner · Joseph N. Dolley · Banking · Small town commerce · Rural finance

In the 1890s, Dolley was among the group of business owners and farmers in Maple Hill who "raised money and contracted with some Chicago slicker to supply us with the necessary quantity of moisture" to bring rain clouds to that summer's endless, burning blue skies. "They arrived at Maple Hill with two barrels of chemicals, a string of iron pipe and some mysterious mechanical doo-dad," and set up their equipment on a platform, as he told the story, years later. Some of his neighbors were so convinced by the rainmakers that they moved furniture and other valuables to the second stories or attics of their homes; farmers moved plows and harvesters to high ground, as the rainmakers set up their equipment out of sight on a platform behind an enclosure and sternly warned people

D. Ress, *The Kansas Blue Sky Act of 1911*,
https://doi.org/10.1007/978-3-031-43831-8_2

to stay away. All that could be seen was an "iron pipe pointed toward the sky" which eventually "began to emit a light milk-colored spray." Dolley and his neighbors waited breathlessly; not a cloud appeared. "The milky spray was cast up for four days and four nights. But there was no sign of rain," Dolley recalled. On the fifth day, he led a delegation to the rain-makers' work site, and ignoring a sign with the firm warning to stay out, discovered that the hucksters had fled in the night. It was not a total loss, despite the money the community had paid. "Not only did we have no flood but we saved others from such a fate because the rain making equipment was left with us," Dolley concluded. In 1911, while testifying before a Kansas state Senate committee about his proposed law to ban inappropriate stock and bond offerings, a state senator asked him what to call the law. Dolley paused for a moment and then "Remembering our experience with the blue sky artists in trying to make rain, I suggested 'the blue sky law.' The name stuck."[1]

Dolley had presented his Blue Sky Act as a way of dealing with frauds, but there is a point about his tale of the rainmakers that he did not stress: the rainmakers, as Dolley said, actually had tried to make rain; they seemed to believe they could. When they failed, they fled; but they left everything behind them. They would not be able to pull the same scam on another town, at least not with the chemicals and unused pipe and "mechanical doo-dad" they had brought with them to Maple Hill. While it is possible that they would have considered that a simply cost of doing business, it might also have reflected a belated realization that a theory sincerely believed in had been disproved and that it was time to move on—before the tar and feathers that would otherwise have been the final scene of this sort of tale. This was, however, not a point that Dolley would stress when telling the story. Yet it would be that gray area between outright fraud and the excessively hopeful that was the focus of the Blue Sky law—fraud, which was one way to unwind a purchase under the *caveat emptor* doctrine, and hope, which flourished when people did not really understand a proposal, as residents of Maple Hill did not understand what causes rain to fall.[2] Paternalism—acting when others cannot look out for their own self-interest—is easier to accept in crisis, whether of drought or failed investment hopes.

Dolley had settled in the hamlet of Maple Hill, Kansas, in 1885 when he quit his life at sea; his last voyage, from New York to Maine to load ice for the long journey to the East Indies, had ended when a gale blowing in from the southwest drove his ship onto the shore. At 3:00 a.m., its bottom stoved in, the ship began to sink. Dolley and the rest of the crew climbed the rigging for what they hoped, with little realistic reason for such hope, would be safety. He and his shipmates clung to the spars for hours, rescued only in the morning, just in time to watch the spars and rigging they had held on to sink into the sea. It was not the first disaster the 26-year old had survived in a nearly a decade of sailing to China and southeast Asia. He had sailed with his ship captain father until his father was killed while crossing Cape Horn; two brothers had died at sea. Though he would say he feared missing the sea when he gave it up, he was later in life more than satisfied by an occasional trip back east to, as he said, smell the salt air, enjoy a clambake, and spend a day or two on a quiet sailing jaunt along the coast.[3] He had had enough of seeing the world.

For his first seventeen years in Kansas, Dolley stayed close to home in Maple Hill and Wabaunsee County. There, he found business dealings were not much like the cargoes his father had brokered for his ship. The busy commerce of Boston, with its scores of merchants and shipowners, created a market where the buyers of goods relied only on their own wits and wariness—where caveat emptor seemed to make sense. Tiny Maple Hill was on what had been in the Pottawatomie Reserve, the thirty miles-square swathe of rolling Kansas prairie ceded to the United States in 1861 to be subdivided into farmsteads and sold to finance the Atkinson, Topeka, and Santa Fe Railroad company.[4] Sales were slow and settlers were few, however, so that in 1882 George Fowler, son of a Kansas City packing house operator, was able to snap up three 640-acre sections and an adjoining 560 acres in smaller parcels on the high ground north of the Mill Creek ford. The first store came two years later, down by Mill Creek. Dolley, on arriving the following year, bought into this venture. But he helped Fowler lobby for a new Chicago, Nebraska, and Kansas Railroad branch line connection across Fowler's high ground holding, away from the creek, which made it possible for Fowler to sell town lots in what would become Maple Hill. Dolley bought a lot there, too, and built his own store and a warehouse in the new town. Dolley eventually "carried a larger stock of goods than is usually found in a small town, being about a $20,000 stock" and nervously expanded his credit business after a brief and unsuccessful experiment running a cash-only business.[5]

After a fire in 1901, he floated a new idea: "J.N. Dolley, recently burned out at Maple Hill, contemplates opening a bank ...Mr. Dolley is the man to start it," a county seat weekly reported, but it would take another five years to launch the Stockgrowers State Bank. Dolley, instead, acted as a non-bank bank: providing credit through his private brokering of farm sales and leases as well as financing crops through his presidency of the Mid-Kansas Milling Company. He bought shares in the newly formed Wabaunsee County Telephone Company and even took a flier far from Maple Hill with an investment in the new P.C.C. Oil and Gas Company, based in Chanute, Kansas. This firm was never able to come close to meeting a promise to deliver gas from its wells; managing barely a quarter of what it had contracted to supply.[6] There was, evidently, a basis for Dolley's later skepticism about oil stock promotions.

Dolley's formal launch into banking, as vice president of the Stockgrowers State Bank, came some four years after he finally entered state politics, winning election to the Kansas House of Representatives in November 1902.[7] He eventually also became president of the Commercial National Bank in Alma, the Wabaunsee County seat.[8] It was not long, moreover, before the new-minted banker—barely three years in the business—and rising politician took on the role of state Banking Commissioner. "Why, I had been in the banking business here in Kansas a good many years before I became bank commissioner," Dolley told the *Saturday Evening Post*, stretching things a bit, as he told the magazine that his experience in the Stockgrowers's Main Street office had informed his push for the Blue Sky Act:

> Every now and then I would hear of one of these swindles—that somebody had lost his money through buying stock in a fake mine, or in a Central American plantation that was nine parts imagination, or in some wonderful investment company that was going to pay forty per cent dividends. Sometimes I knew the man or woman who had been swindled. Of course I thought it was an outrage, but I don't know as it occurred to me then that there was any way to stop it.[9]

It is unlikely that many of Dolley neighbors back in Maple Hill would have enjoyed his recollections of country banking, if they had heard him make the point that many victims of securities swindles "pass for being shrewd and long-headed; people who have amassed some property or money." They were, in Dolley's view, not in fact that sharp. In their inexperience "They are caught by the bait of big dividends promised" and their knowledge of the real world, the world outside the village, was limited, said this man who had seen a bit of the wider world himself—and who had been stung by dreams of dividends from the Chanute gas wells—for otherwise they would have known that: "A new stock company, even if it was honestly promoted and well managed, has a rough road for the first year. Yet here comes an agent and promises 30 percent in dividends."[10]

But perhaps his neighbors did eventually come to know what he thought of them. After the 1909 legislative session ended and Dolley turned his attention not to Maple Hill but rather on his future agenda as Speaker of the House as well as on the re-election of his close political ally, Governor Walter R. Stubbs. He was certain that (as the Topeka *Daily Capital* had predicted) there was "No stopping Dolley in Wabaunsee, where the farmers know him, trust him, believe in him and vote for him," and he missed all the signals that would have warned a more careful listener of impending trouble.[11] He lost what he, and most of the Topeka statehouse crowd, thought was a secure seat in the state House of Representatives. "There was a rebellion in this staunch Republican county against Hon. Dolley," as the *Topeka State Journal*'s "Seen from the Gallery" put it. "Old Republicans who had steadfastly voted the Republican ticket since the days of Populism 'riz up' and elected a democrat ... (with) the claim that Dolley spent his time representing Stubbs rather than Wabaunsee County."[12] The man who for his first seventeen years as their neighbor had seemed content to limit his horizons to little Maple Hill had, after just seven years playing politics, become more than a little swollen headed. There were plenty of folk tales, too, that might have warned of the consequences of that.

However, it was also as Dolley started looking farther afield than Maple Hill that he had come to realize that the kind of miniature economy in which he had prospered was faltering. His tales of city slickers and hayseeds would stress that the businesses those slickers touted "were foreign companies," the looming threat that was a major worry of business owners in the tiny, false front shops of small-town Main Street. To these whispers, it turned out, he had been listening: the menace of the city slicker and the threat posed to trusting, mutually satisfying deals neighbors struck with each other was an ever more prominent theme in the tales that people in the rural mid-continent told one another. In a typical marketing pitch of the day, Dr. J. U. Catudal warned the people of Hays, Kansas, that when they "patronize some foreign physician," they would find those traveling or mail order operators only aimed to "get your note"—an IOU—and then would "give you a little colored medicine... and they are gone ... Give your note. He's gone. Stuck Again." The doctor took such notes, too, despite his chronic trouble getting paid as he continued to treat people and continued to take their IOUs.[13] The doctor trusted because, like any Main Street business in a community like Hays (or Maple Hill), he had to; trust mattered because commerce involved multiple transactions over long periods with neighbors, unlike the instantaneous nature of a purchase under the caveat emptor doctrine.

Buying and selling were not the only transactions done on trust within tiny Kansan communities, either. Businesses in remote communities were necessarily financed locally. Hoping to set up a mill in Ellis County, Kansas, G. M. Cox looked to his future customers for financing help: "Having been urgently requested by numerous farmers of Ellis Co. to put in machinery for making flour … I will accept one load of wheat from all farmers who wish to assist in the enterprise as a LOAN." The idea was that he would sell the flour and use the proceeds to repay farmers for the wheat that they had lent. To secure that, he said he would issue notes to be redeemed in one or two years and said he would pay off any notes in case he could not bring his idea to completion. It took him seven years to secure enough investors.[14]

Small-scale investment by neighbors had been a norm, but one that was already fading. In Dodge City, Kansas, small Main Street merchants joined forces to invest in a new idea: a department store. Each bought shares in the business, and some managed a part of the new, bigger operation. A. D. Smith, manager of the hardware department at the Bargain Store—Dodge City Mercantile Company, to give its more formal name—and one of the department store's owners, had run a small grocery store but decided to use his life savings to buy into the larger Bargain Store venture and try a new line of business. So did grocery and meat department manager Sam Stubbs and his partner in a smaller grocery business, Frank Barkley, who also invested in the business. The store's bookkeeper, W. E. Teare, and the store's eventual landlord bought into the business, too. Their venture eventually drew customers from many miles beyond Dodge City before a fire destroyed it.[15] Although they tried, the Bargain Store's stockholder-operators never could muster the funds locally to rebuild it. The Bargain Store had become a property more valuable than the initial sums invested in, the amount covered by insurance; its replacement was beyond the capabilities of its investors or of the community at large.[16]

Commerce traditionally had had a distinctly sporadic and informal feel in the self-contained economies of small communities in Kansas (and rural places in other states) during the first decade of the twentieth century.

Exchanges often still were a matter of trust, as they had been pretty much since settlers first came. “All persons owing us will confer a favor by settling their account by cash or note,” the Boyer sisters, milliners in tiny Meade Center, Kansas, asked—adding that “We are needing the money to repair our building.”[17] One of the most important transactions of all, the lease of farm in exchange for a third of the crop, was typically not confirmed in writing. While the landlord trusted the tenant to plant and tend and harvest competently, and eventually to deliver that one-third share, the tenant in turn trusted that the landlord had arranged for the necessary work to ensure that the land was adequately watered or drained and that he or she would provide the tools, machinery or horses needed to do the work, that housing would be fit for a family and that, were the tenant to invest in improvements to the farm, he or she could count on working the place for more than the one-year term of the typical lease.

The informality of buying and selling in the miniature economies that Dolley knew so well put a premium on the word of buyers and sellers—on handshake deals as it were—and on the maintenance of neighbors' long-term relationships. Unlike the implicit “I win, you lose” of transactions governed by the *caveat emptor* “buyer beware” rule, or the tales of Yankee peddlers' sharp dealings, transactions could commonly be reconsidered in the tiny towns dotting the plains. So, W. S. Coleman had not kept his own careful records, but instead relied on his customers keeping tallies of their debts, when he asked them to “settle their accounts, either by the payment of money or by making other satisfactory arrangements.”[18] Nor did the fact that he had allowed his cash-short customers to run a tab preclude settling up with yet another promise to pay sometime in the future or reconsideration of the sum owed—those “other satisfactory arrangements.” Obligation to one another could continue long after a transaction.

Still, when it came to investing, Dolley said “local companies with local men behind them engaged in local business about which every man has a chance to know something are a different matter” than a promotion from a traveling stock boomer. This was so, he believed, even if promoters were offering something more real than 50 percent dividends from Mexican plantations or still-to-be-drilled gushers on supposed oil claims. Even in the smallest Kansas community, Dolley said, people ought to remember the lessons of the Santa Fe railway and its several receiverships. For “how many of the men of the promoters and first stockholders who entered via the ground floor made money out of it?” he asked—and answered:

"Not one." That was why, Dolley said, he felt he had to warn "against the promiscuous habits of Kansas people to buy stock from every agent who comes along."[19] Buying shares, even of giant railroads, was simply inappropriate for most Kansans, in Dolley's view.

As important as it was to protect his incompetent neighbors, Dolley was also concerned to keep Kansas money in Kansas. When Kansans invested in out-of-state ventures:

> Not a single pound of merchandise is brought into the State with it; not a single workman is placed on a payroll as a result; not a single natural resource of any community is developed; not a grain is planted; not a steer is added to the herds. It is simply a case of no return for the money. No benefit to anybody within the borders of the State.

Dolley complained.[20] Not too long before pushing for the protection of Kansans' savings through his Blue Sky Act, Dolley supported a concerted campaign by country banks in 1910 to demand cash payments on outstanding notes as a way to secure the necessary resources to finance that year's planting and harvest. Any short-term pain was worth it in order to undercut the eastern banks with their high interest rates, and so give farmers a break at a time when wheat and grain prices were strong. "After a struggle in which it appeared more than once that Wall Street would force another panic similar to the one in 1907, the westerners have won," Dolley commented. "What is more it is believed that the victory will be for all time and that the east never again will dictate whether the western country shall be prosperous." His was a local (or better said, a Kansas-focused) version of the protectionist tariff for imported goods urged by the Progressive Party in its 1912 platform; Dolley, as his hopes for the Republican Party nomination as its candidate for governor faded, briefly became a Bull Mooser that year. That mythical self-sufficiency, so typical of the Maple Hill he had moved to in 1885 and that he still thought he saw from his Topeka office, was exactly what Kansans wanted, Dolley argued. "The west is becoming more and more independent," he declared, for "there is a determination and policy among western men to do their financiering themselves."[21]

But Dolley emphatically did not believe that "financiering" should be unsupervised. Nor did Kansas Governor Stubbs, who reportedly told Dolley: "I want you to examine every bank in the State just as if you were going to buy it. Then supervise them as if you owned them." Both men understood the unspoken point that the Commissioner's post would give Dolley enough time to let him continue as party chairman and manage Stubbs' re-election campaign.[22] The job long had been a sinecure, a way for a politician to afford to stay focused on politics by providing an income that would replace or exceed necessarily neglected business back home.

Dolley was an activist Commissioner, although his first years were marked by accusations of mishandling the collapse of an Abilene bank, by underestimating the shortfall between its assets and what was due depositors to avoid a call on the state's new guaranty fund.[23] He was caught up, too, in a bruising fight that went all the way to the U.S. Supreme Court over reforms of the guaranty fund that had been his most important bill—and his legislative triumph—as Speaker of the Kansas House the year before. Several banks sued in federal court, charging that the law was unconstitutional. While the law did not require banks to participate in the fund, these constitutional challenges charged that it would have the effect of driving them out of business if they did not join in. They also complained that under Dolley's guaranty fund law, the assets of any insolvent bank would be cashed in to repay depositors, instead of being shared among the banks that had paid into the fund, as was the case previously. Both, the banks argued violated the constitutional promise of equal treatment under law, but the U.S. District Court ruled that the banks had not shown their constitutional rights had been infringed and the U.S. Supreme Court agreed.[24]

At the same time, he saw the Commissioner's Office as potentially involving much more than examining bank balance sheets and managing the new guaranty fund. In a speech to the Anti-Horse Thief Association, a private police force he was eyeing as an ally for another publicity initiative, he briefly assumed his old country banker role to ask anyone who had not been swindled in a stock deal to stand—and only one person did. He was, it seems, already thinking about a broader role for the state in regulating financial matters and knew that an alliance with the Anti-Horse Thief Association in a campaign to arrest and convict bank robbers would generate plenty of front page—positive front page—copy across Kansas in 1910 and 1911.[25] In addition to the bank guaranty law fight and its helpful political message that he was looking out for ordinary Kansans, "I ... am fully determined to do everything in my power as Bank commissioner of the state of Kansas to capture, dead or alive, every one of these murderous thugs," he said.[26]

He also announced that he would step in to prevent "undesirables" from buying stock in banks. Anyone buying shares in a state bank would have to have a net worth twice as large as the value of that shareholding, he added. State law required that all the stockholders of a bank had to have combined resources equal to at least twice the capital of the bank—that is, twice the amount of money that was supposed to ensure that depositors could recover their funds. Dolley took a step beyond this: "Every man who purchases stock in a state bank must be worth double liability … I am going to make that rule so rigid that when a man sees a bank is capitalized at $25,000, he will know that the capitalization is really double that amount."[27]

Dolley and Kansan bankers squabbled particularly bitterly over his proposal that banks' interest rates on deposits be capped: he wanted a ceiling of three percent. Bankers, worried about losing deposits, wanted more. Dolley believed that when bankers tried to woo depositors with higher interest rates, they would necessarily turn to riskier loans and investments to cover those higher deposit rates and yield a desired profit. That did not fit his view that a banker was supposed to be "imbued with the sense of responsibility for the welfare of his customers." If as Commissioner he needed to take a firm hand, then so be it, he told the state bankers' association convention shortly after taking office.[28]

In the end, he accepted a compromise: the three percent cap would apply if all banks in a county agreed it, but if they could not, they were free to pay up to four percent to compete more effectively for deposits.[29] Nevertheless, while he and the state's bankers differed as to where the cap should be, they all shared a view that there ought to be a limit on what Kansans should earn on their savings. There was a natural order to saving and borrowing, and whether that was based on a three percent or four percent deposit rate, they all agreed that earning more on savings meant lending at rates that would be unaffordable for farmers and small-town businesses—unless, that is, banks' own profit margins were to shrink. Dolley, though, wanted to do still more to encourage well-ordered rural finance.

In the summer of 1910, then, he launched small new department that had nothing obvious to do with banks at all: a bureau to respond to Kansans' question about stock offerings.[30] "Joe Dolley Is After the Blue Sky Merchants," the Topeka *Daily Capital*, edited by his friend, business associate, and political ally (and eventual rival for governor) Arthur Capper, declared. The story the *Capitol* printed was about letters Dolley had mailed to newspaper editors across the state, asking them to let readers know they could write in to ask if a stock was legitimate or not. "We have made much research," the letter declared, "and are amazed at the enormous amount of money the Kansas people are being swindled out of by these fakers and 'blue sky merchants.' I find that Kansas is literally infested with them." The number of stock boomers trawling the state had climbed by a third in just the past year, he said, adding:

> They are sitting around, and when a man dies and the widow receives her pittance of insurance -- one, two or three thousand dollars, as the case may be, mostly from fraternal insurance -- these thieves show up a few days after the funeral and undertake to sell the widow some of their fake stock, promising her dividends of anywhere from fifteen to fifty per cent per annum.[31]

Notes

1. "Blue Sky Law Named After Drouth," *Topeka State Journal*, October 30, 1935: 9E.
2. A transaction may also be unwound and the buyer reimbursed if the seller granted an express warranty that the goods or services sold were exactly as described at the time of sale.
3. "In the Senate," Ibid., February 18, 1905: 5.
4. Treaty with the Potawatomie Nation, June 5, 1846, 9 Statutes at Large 853; Treaty with the Potawatomie, November 15, 1861, 12 Stat. 1191; Pottawatomie Reserve Lands, Patents No. 1301-2467, Manuscripts Collection 789, Box 755, Kansas State Archives, Topeka.
5. "Dissolution Notice," *The Alma (Kansas) News*, February 27, 1884: 3; Untitled, *Alma Signal*, June 19, 1890: 5: "We Are Now Ready," *Alma Enterprise*, November 6, 1896: 8; "Don't Forget We Sell Insurance," Ibid., June 28, 1901: 1.
6. "Personal Mention," *Alma Enterprise*, April 18, 1902: 8; "Out of Town Notes," *Alma Signal*, May 16, 1902: 4; "Joseph N. Dolley," in Frank W. Blackmar (editor) *Kansas: A Cyclopedia of State History, Embracing Events, Institutions, Industries, Counties, Cities, Towns, Prominent Persons, etc.*, Vol III (Chicago: Standard Publishing, 1912): 176. "A Big Oil Deal," *Topeka State Journal*,

April 28, 1904: 3; "Oil and Gas Meeting," Ibid., April 12, 1906: 7; "Nearly Eighteen Hundred Dollars Worth Less of Gas Purchased," *Chanute (Kansas) Times*, December 13, 1912: 1.

7. "Hanley Is Elected," *Topeka State Journal*, January 23, 1902: 7; "All Are Nominated," *Wichita Daily Eagle*, October 2, 1902: 8; "Bailey Sweeps the State," *Topeka State Journal*, November 5, 1902: 7; "Maple Hill," *Business Directory and History of Wabaunsee County* (Topeka: The Kansas Directory Co, 1907), 73–80. After a term in the House of Representatives, Dolley won election to the state Senate, where, a relative neophyte, he got off to a rough start. An early effort, a proposal to present a silver service to the officers' wardroom of the new battleship USS Kansas, was rejected as a Republican regular thundered: "I don't know that we ought to tax the people of western Kansas who eat out of tin plates with tin spoons to buy a silver service for officers in gold lace and epaulettes." He stumbled when an opponent moved to reconsider passage of a bill to establish a board of control over state mental hospitals and juvenile reformatories: "What bill is that?" Dolley asked; "Senator Dolley looked frightened," the *Topeka State Journal* reported, describing how he nervously looked around for the two Senators who had helped secure passage of the bill. When he awkwardly managed to kill the reconsideration motion, the vote was followed by a wave of laughter at his expense. "No Silver Service," *Topeka State Journal*, February 25, 1905: 14.
8. "Joseph N. Dolly," in *Kansas: A Cyclopedia of State History*: 176.
9. Will Payne "How Kansas Drove out a Den of Thieves, *Saturday Evening Post*, December 2, 1911: 3.
10. "The Plan Works," *Topeka State Journal*, June 9, 1910: 1.
11. "Joseph N. Dolley," in *Kansas: A Cyclopedia:* 177.
12. "Seen from the Gallery," *Topeka State Journal*, January 12, 1911: 9.
13. Notice (no headline) *Hays (Kansas) Free Press*, October 8, 1904: 1; Notice, Ibid., August 13, 1910: 5.
14. "A New Grist Mill" *Hays Free Press,* July 21, 1900: 1; "Local News," Ibid., November 9, 1907: 4.
15. "Bargain Store Destroyed by Fire Early Monday Evening," *The Globe-Republican* (Dodge City, Kansas) November 4, 1909: 1.

16. "To Build at Once," Ibid., November 11, 1909: 1; "Bargain Store," Ibid., November 25, 1909: 1; "Barkley Grocery," Ibid. December 9, 1909: 1 and "Cut Price Grocery," Ibid., 8.
17. Notice, no headline, *Meade County News*, January 4, 1906: 1.
18. "Notice to Debtors," *Goodland (Kansas) Republic*. July 27, 1906: 1.
19. "The Plan Works," *Topeka State Journal*, June 9, 1910: 1.
20. "Saving the People's Money," *Ticker and Investment Digest*, August 1910: 157.
21. "To Go It Alone," *Topeka State Journal*, October 13, 1910: 5.
22. Isaac Marcosson, "Barring Out the Stock Thieves," *Munsey's Magazine*, February 1912: 678.
23. "Management of Bank Matter Criticized," *Abilene (Kansas) Weekly Reflector*, December 8, 1910: 1.
24. Assaria State Bank of Assaria, Citizens Bank of Axtell, et al. v Joseph N. Dolly 219 U.S. 121 (U.S. Supreme Court, 1911) "Management of the Bank Matter Criticized," *Abilene Weekly Reflector*, December 8, 1910: 1.
25. Marcosson, "Barring Out the Stock Thieves," 678.
26. "A Price of $1,000 on Robbers' Heads," *Topeka Daily Capital*, December 18, 1910: 1. His plan was actually to direct Kansas bankers to join the Anti-Horse Thief Association and put up the money for a $1,000 reward for any arrests; the Commissioner's office itself would play no other role.
27. "Look Up the Purchasers," *Topeka Daily Capita*l, April 23, 1911: 1.
28. Joseph N. Dolley, "The New Kansas Banking Laws," *Topeka State Journal*, January 4, 1911: 1 (reporting on his speech to the 22nd Annual Convention of the Kansas Bankers Association in May 1909).
29. "Dolley Fixes Rate," *Topeka State Journal*, March 11, 1911: 6; "Banks May Agree to Pay Only 3% Interest," *Topeka Daily Capital*, March 19, 1911: 18.
30. "The Plan Works," *Topeka State Journal*, June 9, 1910: 1; "Would Guard Investors," *Chanute (Kansas) Times*, December 23, 1910: 6; "Goes with Rush," *Topeka State Journal*, February 11, 1911: 6.
31. "Joe Dolley Is After the Blue Sky Merchants," *Topeka Daily Capita*l, December 22, 1910: 4.

Bibliography

Anonymous. 1884. "Dissolution Notice," *The Alma (Kansas) News*, February 27: 3.

———. 1890. Untitled, *Alma Signal*, June 19: 5.

———. 1896. "We Are Now Ready," *Alma Enterprise*, November 6: 8.

———. 1900. "A New Grist Mill" *Hays (Kansas) Free Press,* July 21, 1900: 1.

———. 1901. "Don't Forget We Sell Insurance," *Alma Enterprise*, June 28: 1.

———. 1902a. "Hanley is Elected," *Topeka State Journal*, January 23: 7.

———. 1902b. "Personal Mention," *Alma Enterprise*, April 18: 8.

———. 1902c. "Out of Town Notes," *Alma Signa*l, May 16: 4.

———. 1902d."All Are Nominated," *Wichita Daily Eagle*, October 2: 8.

———. 1902e. "Bailey Sweeps the State," *Topeka State Journal*, November 5: 7.

———. 1904a. "A Big Oil Deal," *Topeka State Journal*, April 28: 3.

———. 1904b. Notice (no headline) *Hays Free Press*, October 8: 1.

———. 1905. "In the Senate," *Topeka State Journal*, February 18: 5.

———. 1906a. Notice, no headline, *Meade County News*, January 4: 1.

———. 1906b. "Oil and Gas Meeting," *Topeka State Journal*, April 12:7.

———. 1906c. "Notice to Debtors," *Goodland (Kansas) Republic*, July 27: 1.

———. 1907a. "Local News," *Hays Free Press*, November 9: 4

———. 1907b. "Maple Hill", *Business Directory and History of Wabaunsee County*. Topeka: The Kansas Directory Co.

———. 1909a. "Bargain Store Destroyed by Fire Early Monday Evening," *The Globe-Republican* (Dodge City, Kansas), November 4: 1.

———. 1909b. "To Build at Once," *The Globe-Republican*, November 11: 1.

———. 1909c. "Bargain Store," *The Globe-Republican*, November 25: 1.

———. 1909d. "Barkley Grocery" and "Cut Price Grocery," *The Globe-Republican,* December 9: 1, 8.

———. 1910a. "The Plan Works," *Topeka State Journal*, June 9: 1.

———. 1910b. "Saving the People's Money," *Ticker and Investment Digest*, August: 157.

———. 1910c. Notice, *Hays Free Press*, August 13: 5.

———. 1910d. "To Go It Alone," *Topeka State Journal*, October 13: 5.

———. 1910e. "A Price of $1,000 on Robbers' Heads," *Topeka Daily Capital*, December 18: 1.

———. 1910f. "Joe Dolley Is After the Blue Sky Merchants," *Topeka Daily Capital*, December 22: 4.

———. 1910g. "Would Guard Investors," *Chanute (Kansas) Times*, December 23: 6.

———. 1911a. "Seen from the Gallery," *Topeka State Journal*, January 12: 9.

———. 1911b. "Goes with Rush," *Topeka State Journal*, February 11: 6.

———. 1911c. "Dolley Fixes Rate," *Topeka State Journal*, March 11: 6.

———. 1911d. "Banks May Agree to Pay Only 3% Interest," *Topeka Daily Capital*, March 19: 18.
———. 1911e. "Look Up the Purchasers," *Topeka Daily Capital*, April 23: 1.
———. 1912a. "Joseph N. Dolley," in Frank W. Blackmar (editor) 1912. *Kansas: A Cyclopedia of State History, Embracing Events, Institutions, Industries, Counties, Cities, Towns, Prominent Persons, etc.*, III: 176–177.
———. 1912b. "Nearly Eighteen Hundred Dollars Worth Less of Gas Purchased," *Chanute (Kansas) Times*, December 13: 1.
———. 1935. "Blue Sky Law Named After Drouth," *Topeka State Journal*, October 30: 9E.
Assaria State Bank of Assaria, Citizens Bank of Axtell, et al. v Joseph N. Dolly 219 U.S. 121 (U.S. Supreme Court, 1911).
Dolley, Joseph N. 1911. "The New Kansas Banking Laws," *Topeka State Journal*, January 4: 1.
Marcosson, Isaac. 1912. "Barring Out the Stock Thieves," *Munsey's Magazine*, February: 674–680.
Payne, Will. 1911. "How Kansas Drove out a Den of Thieves," *Saturday Evening Post*, December 2: 3–5.

CHAPTER 3

Caveat Emptor and Selling Stocks: Mr. Thompkins Comes to Town

Abstract There were no effective legal remedies against the promoters of dubious share offerings, just as for most American commerce there were no remedies for disappointed buyers because most American judges' adherence to the *caveat emptor* doctrine was so firm—firmer than in the English courts in which the concept first arose. Rural Kansans, used to a different model of commerce, and where judges were more skeptical of caveat emptor, felt especially victimized by stock promoters and Kansas Banking Commissioner Joseph N. Dolley would tap into those sentiments with his Blue Sky Act.

Keywords Securities sales · Fraud · Regulation · Caveat emptor

Pause for moment on the doorstep of what Kansas State Bank Commissioner Dolley described as an especially pretty little cottage to hear Mr. Thompkins say when the widow opened her front door: "Your late husband was such a fine man" and assure her that he knew him: a hard worker, family man, and a brother member of the fraternal order. Thompkins rattled off a few other fake recollections of her late husband based on what he had gleaned from the obituary. Then, he mentioned that the deceased machinist had, as it happened, shown some interest in the Pan-American Plantations Company. It was, Thompkins continued, so sad that

D. Ress, *The Kansas Blue Sky Act of 1911*,
https://doi.org/10.1007/978-3-031-43831-8_3

he had died so unexpectedly because he surely would have invested in the company. So sad, too, that the old-fashioned ways to hold one's savings that were possible in a little Kansas railroad town brought such small returns. He himself was not exactly a rich man but he was putting every cent he could make into Pan-American Plantations stock and counting upon being a millionaire shortly, spinning a tale for the naïve young widow of unbelievably rich lands to the south. Pan-American's holdings were sure to yield annual dividends of 50 cents for each dollar invested in company stock, he declared.[1]

For the young widow, Thompkins' pitch, stated with such authority and apparent knowledge, sounded so much better than the suggestion from the secretary of the local building and loan society that she use the $2,000 to pay off the remaining $600 on the cottage's mortgage and invest the rest in building and loan society shares, Dolley noted in his tale. Those shares would be enough to yield her $5 a month, the secretary had told her. "It isn't much," the building and loan man said, "but it will be absolutely safe. Perhaps I can find something later that will be just as safe and bring you a better return." But there was nothing in that small Kansas town to match the $1,000 a year that Mr. Thompkins dangled before her. In the end, as required for the story to reach its necessary moral, the young widow did not go downtown and did not pay off her mortgage. She swapped her check for a "beautifully lithographed certificate for 2,000 shares of Pan-American Plantations stock that wasn't worth what it cost to have it printed," as Dolley's little parable described it. Thompkins cashed the check, and a half hour later was on a train out of town. A year later, the widow's money gone, her home lost, she and her three children were living in a shack on the edge of town. There, she bent over a washtub six days a week over a washtub, trying to make a living as a washerwoman.[2]

The various Mr. Thompkins working Kansan towns and farms to sell junk securities had a system, Dolley concluded. The stock boomers watched real estate transfers recorded in county courthouses and often reported in newspapers, with the idea that a farmer or landlord who sold a farm, or a widow who sold lot in town, was a possible investor. They watched obituaries, as Mr. Thompkins had, and in doing "they reaped a rich harvest," Dolley explained.[3] The message they brought to their targeted victims was always one of marvels—but marvels not impossible to imagine, especially in a decade that seemed full of marvels only recently made concrete if not yet seen in Kansan hamlets: flying like a bird, thanks to an airplane; hearing distant voices in the air with a radio-set. The $1,000 a year income that Mr. Thompkins promised in return for that Kansas widow's $2,000 insurance check was to come from a tropical garden where exotic luxuries so costly in places like Maple Hill—coffee, oranges, bananas, pineapple, vanilla, and rubber—flourished. It was a vision of riches delightful to contemplate for anyone who labored over a backyard vegetable plot in semi-arid central Kansas or worriedly watched the sky for signs of rain as the wheat crop withered.

Whether the sales pitch stressed natural resources as Pan-American Plantations had or the novel wonders of electricity or radio tales of previously barely imagined possibilities made swallowing the unlikeliest promises of profit painlessly easy, Dolley's tales of city slickers and hayseeds were meant as warnings, just tales of clever frontier types like the Yankee peddler Fred Griswold warned nineteenth-century Americans that *caveat emptor*—the buyer beware rule—governed all buying and selling. Griswold could outwit even a judge who traded him an old grindstone by swapping the heavy, almost worn-out stone for a newborn bull calf in the next valley and then selling the calf back to the judge for twenty times its worth. "Why judge," said the squire who swapped the calf to Griswold for the grindstone, when he spotted the calf in question "I sold him that calf a short time ago for a grindstone!"[4] And there was nothing the judge—a judge of all people—could do but laugh, a bit ruefully—and never try to palm off a worn-out grindstone again.

For the judge knew that the rule of law was *caveat emptor*: buyer beware. Still, while buyer's remorse may seem an eternal element of commerce, *caveat emptor* is not. The moment when buyer and seller agree is, at least in economic theory but perhaps only in theory, a moment when each is satisfied. In theory, the price is fair, or better stated, is the best that can be realized by the seller. In theory, that price is the best that can be negotiated by the buyer—that famous intersection of demand and supply curves. Yet the process of exchange involves more than the moment the deal is struck; it starts sooner than the agreement on price, with marketing, assessment, and often negotiation, it ends well after the item at issue is handed over, with satisfaction or disappointment or resignation over time on the part of both parties. The familiar feeling of buyer's remorse—that, upon reconsideration, the purchase was not really what was wanted, that its features had not been examined with sufficient care, that the decision to buy was reached in too much haste—makes clear a point that the usual theories about markets miss, for commerce is not always an instantaneous event, a matter of one deal struck with each party moving on, but can be instead relationship that continues over more or less time.

The founding document of most European law (though not Anglo-American common law), the Roman Emperor Justinian's *Corpus Juris Civilis* codification, recognized this providing that when buyers and sellers "differ either as to the price, or as to something else connected with the sale, it will be incomplete."[5] The consequence is that "if ... the vendor does not furnish the purchaser with what is required, judgment shall be rendered against him."[6] *Caveat emptor*, in contrast, does not allow for a such after-the-sale resolution of any disappointment, unless as a result of bargaining over terms of the sale an express warranty is agreed. In this, it overturned traditional commercial practice in medieval English versions of the kind of miniature, self-contained economy Dolley had known in Maple Hill. Both in medieval England and early twentieth-century Kansas resolving a disappointed buyer's complaint involved a balancing of the interests of both buyer and seller, as well as creditor and debtor.[7] *Caveat emptor* only emerged as a common law doctrine in the seventeenth century, in a Court of Exchequer decision about the sale of a supposed bezoar stone, an animal concretion that many believed had magic powers. Because the disappointed buyer did not allege a breach of warranty in his lawsuit, he had no case "although he is deceived, for caveat emptor," the justices ruled in this case.[8] It is this decision that is the basis of the Anglo-American caveat emptor rule, although in fact the buyer went back to court and won damages from the seller. It is only this extremely uncertain ground, a disputed sale of a bezoar stone, that the dictate "*caveat emptor*" was founded—and founded even though the disappointed buyer eventually got his money back.[9]

The *caveat emptor* rule troubled English legal scholars and judges ever since. Case law rarely used the term; in one case, where it was mentioned, Lord Chief Justice Ellenborough settled a dispute by ordering the seller to repay part of what he had received, blithely declaring: "Our decision will not clash with the rule, *caveat emptor*, for here both parties were under a mutual error."[10] American judges, however, developed a more sweeping faith in the rule of buyer beware.[11] In what would become the primary American caveat emptor case, Chancellor James Kent of the New York Supreme Court of Judicature (and perhaps the leading American legal commentator of the early nineteenth century) would write that if not for the bezoar stone case—to be precise, the first decision, for Kent seems not to have heard of the second case where the buyer was repaid—and an otherwise rarely cited 1802 English Court of King's Bench decision involving a sale of spoiled hops, "I confess I should be overcome by the reasoning" of Justinian's civil law approach.[12] His ruling came in a decision about a dispute over the shipment of "brazilleto wood" (*Haematoxylum brasiletto,* or Mexican logwood) that turned out to be only "peachum"—trash. Even though Justinian's Digest "gives the very case of selling vitiated wood" to hold a seller "responsible in every case for a latent defect," Kent held that caveat emptor "has been well and elegantly vindicated ... as most happily reconciling the claims of convenience with the duty of good faith." The reason is that "It requires the purchaser to apply his attention to those particulars which may be supposed within the reach of his observation and judgment." The American style of commerce, in short, required buyers and sellers to use their wits, as Griswold would, and as the Pennsylvania judge had not.[13]

Over time, any inclination Kent may have had toward empathy with the disappointed buyer faded. In his *Commentaries on American Law*, Kent held firmly that the law should "not go to the romantic length of giving indemnity against the consequences of indolence and folly" for "The maxim of caveat emptor and that other maxim, *vigilantibus et non dormientibus jura subveniunt*, (rights relieve those who are awake and not asleep) ... are replete with sound and practical wisdom."[14] Americans, in this tale they told about themselves, managed their affairs prudently. In the market, whether as buyer or seller, they saw themselves as clever operators: the sharp-witted peddlers of folklore, like Griswold. *Caveat emptor*, in American courts and in American commerce, was more about Americans' image of themselves than it was about jurisprudence.

This interpretation was not so much the case in Kansas. Trust in neighbor-to-neighbor dealings still mattered—at least to juries in remote communities. So, the Kansas Supreme Court said a jury ought to decide if a naïve tailor, who thought to make a quick profit financing a farmer's corn crop, had been fairly dealt with when a lower court judge had bluntly directed the tailor to pay up; caveat emptor was not sufficient grounds to remove the case from the jury's review.[15] A Reno County, Kansas, jury ruled that Nathan Boam had been shortchanged when he decided to close out his tailoring and laundry business and the buyers did not reimburse him for value of inventory acquired, once they had cleared his debts (mostly purchases on account, made on trust, with no documentation). Here, there was, the Supreme Court justices sighed, nothing they could do about a jury's finding of fact.[16] The Kansan justices, however, would rule that a buyer could refuse to pay in a chase where a Kansas City manufacturer of oil drilling supplies delivered a tank that leaked (because the wooden staves were "sappy" and improperly seasoned).[17] The justices also made a point of holding that "the doctrine of *caveat emptor* does not apply" in a wrongful death case where a restauranter tenant and his landlord were sued after a teenage employee fell to her death in a poorly covered cistern. The court held that the landlord could not claim immunity by claiming *caveat emptor* applied when leasing property with a dangerous defect.[18]

Griswold could fool a judge by fast talk about a calf, and with that popular tale and its healthy dose of humor at the expense of a local big shot, could also help confirm the legal rule of *caveat emptor*, but in Dolley's day, goods—and offerings of stocks and bonds—could come to the people of little Kansas towns that were not as easy to evaluate as a calf or grindstone. This, too, made *caveat emptor* seem even less justified. In places like Great Bend, Kansas, where the weekly *Barton County Democrat* had breathlessly reported on a wonderful expansion of the telephone and radio in the form of wireless telephones (some eighty years before the first would ever arrive), sales agents for the United Wireless Telegraph Company promised that isolated towns far out on the western Kansas plains would be the company's first stations. But they were in those towns not so much to test demand for an invention that did not yet exist as to "give any one who desires an opportunity to purchase stock."[19]

It was a familiar come-on, that promise of modern (or even science fiction) service in return for buying dubious securities. Over just one feverish spring, in 1905, the people of Medicine Lodge and surrounding Barber County, Kansas were overwhelmed with pitches from promoters of four different, but equally unlikely, railroad proposals. The first was for a still-to-be-formed railroad based centered in tiny Great Bend, Kansas. A another group competed for their money to build a railroad directly linking Medicine Lodge to California. There was a second Great Bend-based venture and, finally, a line that promised to route its Denver to the Gulf of Mexico line through Medicine Lodge if only, as with all the other promotions, Barton County residents bought bonds. While "it is hard to estimate the value of this stock," the *Barber County Index* noted, commenting on the Denver road proposal, "in similar cases it has been known to sell for par after the road has been in operation for several years." When the line was finally built, however, "The service on the new road extends only from Kiowa to Medicine Lodge and it is the most miserable that could be conceived," arriving at 1 a.m. and leaving at 3:30 a.m. and "misses oftener than it connects," with the eastern mail train, the newspaper complained.[20]

Henry Harrison Tucker Jr. promised his proposed 300 barrel-a-day Uncle Sam Oil Co. refinery would drive John D. Rockefeller's Standard Oil Company out of Kansas, while promising dividends that in one year would exceed what people spent buying his shares. The refinery was in fact too dilapidated a condition to operate, as the company's bankruptcy trustee found just two years later.[21] Kansans who bought shares, thinking a tiny refinery (Rockefeller's main refinery was processing 36,000 barrels a day in the 1890s) did not realize that the presence of other, smaller independent refineries had not threatened Standard's control of the oil market. They just saw Tucker as a monopoly-fighting knight.

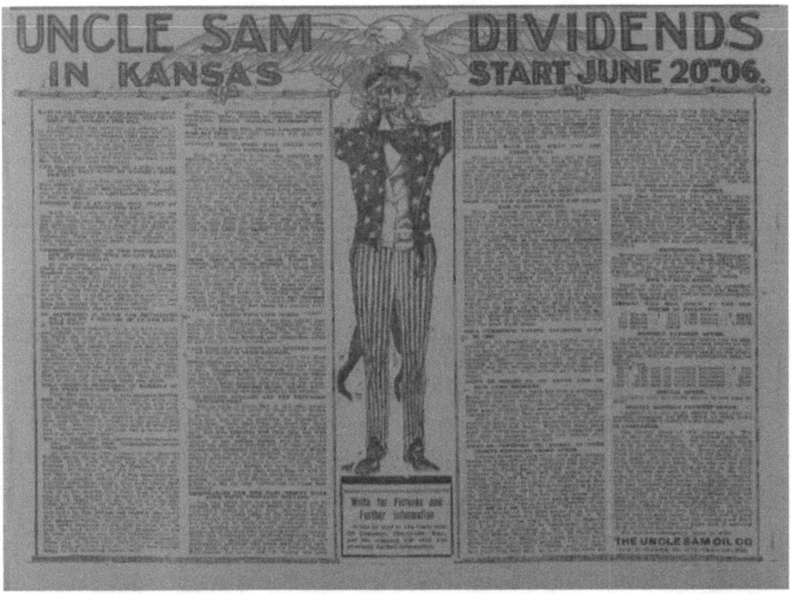

Uncle Sam Oil is from the *Topeka State Journal* April 11, 1906

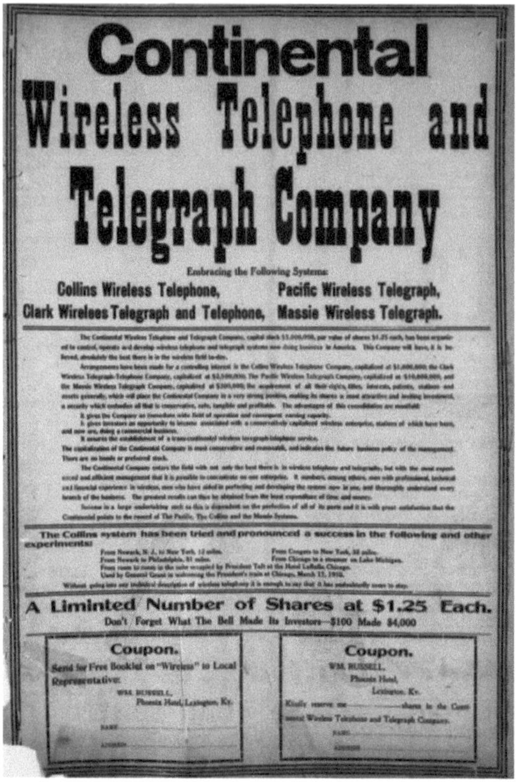

Continental Wireless from *The Bourbon News*, a defunct weekly newspaper, from July 1, 1910

Small-town business owners who rarely traveled thought the idea of a vending machine that sold travel insurance seemed like a sure thing. Kansas City promoter James Armstrong and Great Bend banker J. George Brinkman, "well and favorably known" even 120 miles away in Garden City, convinced scores of small-town business owners across the western part of the state to put money into the idea. In Garden City, he took in $40,000 from thirty-five men. Once it was clear that no dividends were coming, some of the Garden City victims hired a Pinkerton detective to track Armstrong down and convinced a judge to attach land he owned in Ness County to recover some but not all of the money they lost.[22] Despite the certainty most American judges found in the *caveat emptor* rule, Kansans were somewhat more willing override it, after the fact of a sale that disappointed.

Selling stock, not refining oil or underwriting insurance was the point of these businesses, as it was for the railroad promoters flocking to Medicine Lodge and other tiny towns of the mid-continent. Kansans' newfound prosperity after years of hard times made the state a tempting target for stock promoters. Deposits in state-chartered banks increased nearly fivefold in the first decade of the twentieth century, to $90 million; national banks had another $60 million. "That's fat picking," Dolley told the *Saturday Evening Post* before recalling an incident soon after launching the advisory bureau when an old farmer he knew stopped by his Banking Commission office. "He'd sold his Kansas farm and had the money in the bank. A couple of smooth gentlemen came along" and convinced him to buy into a New Mexican irrigation scheme—a stock promotion that Dolley's successor as Banking Commissioner shut down and that eventually landed the promotor, Don Moun Day in prison for mail fraud. The farmer invested, but after waiting months for his dividends, took Dolley's advice to go and look at the land. The old man "walked half a day through the sagebrush, and then climbed some bare, mountainous hills until his wind gave out. The land he'd invested in was still higher up. The only way to irrigate it would be from the moon," Dolley said. "[A]s the law went there seemed nothing to do by way of protecting him from losing his money; but I made up my mind I'd do something."[23]

Notes

1. Marcosson, "Barring Out the Stock Thieves": 678.
2. Ibid.
3. Ibid.
4. "The Yankee Peddler or; How to Make a Fortune," *Washington Almanack* (Philadelphia: R. Wilson Desilver, 1849): 32-33, cited Mary-Lou Hinman, "The Yankee Peddler: His Role in American Folklore and Fiction," Ph.D. dissertation, University of Connecticut, 1975, 53-54.
5. Digest, Book 18, title 1, section 9. https://droitromain.univ-grenoble-alpes.fr/Anglica/D18_Scott.htm#V.
6. Digest, Book 21, title 1, sections. 1, 29, 33 and 49. https://droitromain.univ-grenoble-alpes.fr/Anglica/D21_Scott.htm#V.

7. Berwick Gild Statutes, for instance, said that if a buyer of any item found the purchase to be of worse quality than promised, the seller was to amend matters as a panel of local men dictated, Mary Bateson, *Selden Society: Borough Customs*, Vol. 2 (London: Bernard Quaritch, 1906): 182.
8. Chandelor v. Lopus, Cro. Jac. 4, 79 Eng. Rep. 3 (Court of Exchequer, 1603).
9. There were actually two cases; in the first, most commonly cited, Chandelor v. Lopus, Cro. Jac. 4, 79 Eng. Rep. 3 (Court of Exchequer, 1603), the court dismissed the matter on procedural grounds. The second, while specially declaring deceit was not grounds for recovery because of *caveat emptor* while nevertheless awarding damages, is found in an MSS volume of case reports from the first ten years of James 1 and was detailed in the "Chandelor v. Lopus," *Harvard Law Review*, Vol. 8, No. 5 (December 1894): 282-284; the lawyers' arguments are on 283, judges' views on 284.
10. Cox and others v. Prentice, 3 M. & S. 344; 105 Eng. Rep. 641 (1815), at 345. There were surprisingly few caveat emptor cases; the lack of a vendor's duty is an element in Springwell v. Allen, 2 East 448 (1681) involving title of ownership in a horse and Mew v Russel 89 ER 942 (1682), and over an estimation of the yield of timber was after Chandelor v. Lopus the ones usually cited in American judges' opinions.
11. See, e.g., Sweet v. Cilgage, 20 Johns. 190 (Supreme Court of Judicature of New York, 1822) which held *caveat emptor* barred recovery when a seller falsely described a cargo of kelp as barilla, a more valuable seaweed. Similarly, a buyer of misdescribed blue paint could not recover even after the seller acknowledged when challenged that the paint was not blue. Borrekins v. Bevan, 3 Raule 23 (Pennsylvania Supreme Court, 1831). Despite the common law exception for foodstuffs, anchored in a statute dating back to Henry VII and confirmed by Kent as well as in leading English cases, a New York merchant would be out of luck when he sought damages after finding much of the lot of 194 barrels of beef he had purchased was spoiled and inedible: "*Caveat emptor*, and not *caveat venditor*, is the rule of the common law; and that is our law," New York's Supreme Court of Judicature chief justice Greene Bronson held, Moses v Mead, 1 Denio 378 (Supreme Court of Judicature of New York, 1845) at 385. While fraud entitled the

victim of a fake mining deal to recover his money, a majority of the U.S. Supreme Court held William R. Smith v Guy Richards, 38 U.S. 26 (U.S. Supreme Court, 1839), Justice Joseph Story, whose *Commentaries on the Constitution* were basic texts for American jurisprudence through the nineteenth century wrote that *caveat emptor* should apply since the mine promoter was "the victim, if you please, of a heated and deluded imagination, indulging in golden dreams, but in this respect he is in the same predicament" as the buyer. Ibid., at 44. The Supreme Court was firmer on the buyer beware rule when it overturned a lower court ruling that custom in some businesses could trump caveat emptor. The case involved a large shipment of bales of wool, and the bales had been packed with rotten fleeces in the middle. In the wool trade, the trial court judge had ruled, the custom was that when wool was sold in bales and later found to be unsatisfactory, the seller and buyer should agree on compensation—it was an inconvenient interference with commerce to say baled lots of wool (or, for that matter, cotton) could be properly inspected in time to strike a bargain. But common law, Justice David Davis wrote for the Supreme Court, was clear: "No principle of the common law has been better established, or more often affirmed, both in this country and in England, than that in sales of personal property… the maxim of caveat emptor applies." For "requiring the purchaser to take care of his own interests, has been found best adapted to the wants of trade in the business transactions of life." Barnard v. Kellogg, 77 U.S. 383 (U.S. Supreme Court, 1869) at 388.

12. Seixas and Seixas v Wood, 2 Cai R 48, at 55 (New York Supreme Court of Judicature, 1804). The 1802 case, Parkinson v Lee, affirmed caveat emptor but only after Justice Sir Simon Le Blanc, after first agreeing with the trial jury that heard the matter that the buyer of £200 worth of hops that turned out to be rotten should be paid damages, changed his mind on the appeal. Parkinson v Lee, 2 East 314 (Court of King's Bench, 1802), at 322, 324.
13. Seixas and Seixas v Wood at 55.
14. James Kent, *Commentaries on American law*, Vol. 2 (New York, 1836): 633, 637.
15. Abmeyer v First National Bank of Horton 76 Kan. 877, 92 P. 1109 (Kansas Supreme Court, 1907) The tailor, B.F. Abmeyer, had a notion to make some more money by dealing in grain,

while C.A. Wright, a Jackson County tenant farmer Abmeyer knew, needed funds to carry him over until he could harvest his corn. As the two inspected one of Wright's fields, the farmer said that he expected to harvest 1,300 bushels, worth $494 based on the pre-harvest price then quoted by nearby elevators. Wright proposed that Abmeyer write him a promissory note to pay $400 to purchase the corn; Abmeyer would net a $94 profit without needing to put up any of the $400 until after the corn was sold. Wright then cashed in the note with a friend in the next county, Alex Dunn, Jr., vice president of the First National Bank of Horton, although Dunn had already declined to make a loan against the corn crop. When Wright harvested only 431 bushels, Abmeyer was caught short and couldn't pay Dunn's bank the note. Although Justice Clark Allen Smith noted that upholding the jury's finding did not mean the caveat emptor rule should not have applied, there was in fact at least some precedent in common law holding that the purchase and sale of financial instruments was not subject to the caveat emptor rule, as U.S. Supreme Court Justice Edward Douglas White noted in a case involving the sale of invalidated state of Louisiana bonds, Meyer v. Richards, 163 U.S. 385 (U.S. Supreme Court, 1896) at 415, citing Jones v. Ryde, 5 Taunt. 488, (1814) Wilkinson v. Johnson, 3 B. & C. 428, (1824,) Young v. Cole, 3 Bing. N.C. 724, (1827), Lambert v. Heath, 15 M. & W. 486, (1846) and Gompertz v. Bartlett, 2 El. & Bl. 849 (1853).

16. Boam et al. v Cohen et al. 94 Kan. 42, 145 P. 559 (Kansas Supreme Court, 1915) at 560.
17. Fairbanks, Morse & Co. v Walker, 76 Kan 903 (Kansas Supreme Court, 1907).
18. Bailey et al. v Kelly, 86 Kan 911 (Kansas Supreme Court, 1912) at 1028.
19. "Wireless Station Soon," *The Globe-Republican* (Dodge City, Kansas) February 18 1909: 1; "Be a Representative," *Barton County Democrat* (Great Bend, Kansas) January 22 1909: 8.
20. "To Vote Bonds," and "North and South Railroad Again," *Barber County Index*, April 26, 1905: 1; "Sharon Items," ibid., May 3, 1905: 5; "President Lindley," ibid., May 31, 1905: 1; "Three and Three," ibid., June 7, 1905: 1; "To Vote Bonds," ibid., July 19, 1905: 1; "Small Individually," ibid., September 6, 1905: 1; "The Bond Vote," ibid., November 15, 1905: 1; "A Public Obligation,"

ibid., November 20, 1907:1; "Bonds are Voted," ibid., December 1, 1909:1; "Railroad Meeting at Aetna," ibid., April 13, 1910: 1.

21. "In Fight to Win," *Topeka State Journal*, March 20, 1905: 1; U.S. Census 1910, Vol. 11, Mines and Quarries, Table 24: 280; "Makes Poor Case," *Topeka State Journal*, November 26, 1907: 1; $40,000 Dividend, No. 2, Is Guaranteed," *Topeka State Journal*, July 5, 1906: 5.
22. "Must Pay It Back," *Topeka State Journal*, October 25, 1909: 3.
23. Will Payne "How Kansas Drove Out a Den of Thieves, *Saturday Evening Post*, December 2, 1911: 3.

Bibliography

Abmeyer v First National Bank of Horton 76 Kan. 877, 92 P. 1109 (Kansas Supreme Court, 1907).

Anonymous. 1849. "The Yankee Peddler or; How to Make a Fortune," in *Washington Almanack* Philadelphia, R. Wilson Desilver: 32–33.

——— 1894, "Chandelor v. Lopus," *Harvard Law Review*, 8: 282–284.

——— 1905a "In Fight to Win," *Topeka State Journal*, March 20: 1.

——— 1905b "To Vote Bonds," and "North and South Railroad Again," *Barber County Index* (Medicine Lodge, Kansas) April 26: 1.

——— 1905c "Sharon Items," *Barber County Index*, May 3: 5.

——— 1905d "President Lindley" *Barber County Index*, May 31: 1.

——— 1905e "Three and Three," *Barber County Index*, June 7: 1.

——— 1905f "To Vote Bonds." *Barber County Index*, July 19: 1.

——— 1905g "Small Individually," *Barber County Index*, , September 6: 1.

——— 1905h "The Bond Vote," *Barber County Index*, November 15: 1.

——— 1906 "$40,000 Dividend, No. 2, Is Guaranteed," *Topeka State Journal*, July 5: 5.

——— 1907a "A Public Obligation," *Barber County Index*, , November 20: 1.

——— 1907b "Makes Poor Case," *Topeka State Journal*, November 26: 1.

——— 1909a "Be a Representative," *Barton County Democrat* (Great Bend, Kansas) January 22: 8.

——— 1909b "Wireless Station Soon," *The Globe-Republican* (Dodge City, Kansas) February 18: 1.

——— 1909a "Must Pay It Back," *Topeka State Journal*, October 25: 3.

——— 1909b "Bonds Are Voted," *Barber County Index*, December 1: 1.

——— 1910 "Railroad Meeting at Aetna," *Barber County Index*, April 13: 1.

Bailey et al. v Kelly, 86 Kan 911 (Kansas Supreme Court, 1912).

Bateson, Mary. 1906. *Selden Society: Borough Customs*. London: Bernard Quaritch.

Boam et al. v Cohen et al 94 Kan. 42 (Kansas Supreme Court, 1915).

Borrekins v. Bevan, 3 Raule 23 (Pennsylvania Supreme Court, 1831).

Corpus Juris Civilis Digest, Book 18, title 1, section 9. https://droitromain.univ-grenoble-alpes.fr/Anglica/D18_Scott.htm#V (accessed September 1 2021) and Digest, Book 21, title 1, sections 1, 29, 33 and 49. https://droitromain.univ-grenoble-alpes.fr/Anglica/D21_Scott.htm#V (accessed September 1 2021).

Chandelor v. Lopus, Cro. Jac. 4, 79 Eng. Rep. 3 (Court of Exchequer, 1603).

Cox and others v. Prentice, 3 M. & S. 344; 105 Eng. Rep. 641 (Court of King's Bench, 1815).

Fairbanks, Morse & Co. v Walker, 76 Kan 903 (Kansas Supreme Court, 1907)

Kent, James. 1836. *Commentaries on American law*, Vol, 2 New York: Clayton and Van Norden (3rd Edition).

Marcosson, Isaac. 1912 "Barring Out the Stock Thieves," *Munsey's Magazine*, February: 674–680.

Mew v Russel 89 ER 942 (Court of Exchequer, 1682).

Moses v Mead, 1 Denio 378 (Supreme Court of Judicature of New York, 1845).

Parkinson v Lee, 2 East 314 (Court of King's Bench, 1802).

Payne, Will. 1911. "How Kansas Drove Out a Den of Thieves, *Saturday Evening Post*, December 2: 3–5.

Seixas and Seixas v Wood, 2 Cai R 48 (New York Supreme Court of Judicature, 1804).

Springwell v. Allen, 2 East 448 (Court of Exchequer, 1681).

Sweet v. Cilgage, 20 Johns. 190 (Supreme Court of Judicature of New York, 1822).

CHAPTER 4

The First Securities Law: Kansas Goes After the "Fakirs"

Abstract Reservations about the paternalism inherent in Joseph N. Dolley's Blue Sky Act emerged during the Kansas legislature's debates, while Dolley's supposed Progressive Republican allies split over the issue; while some joined him, others did not, and some rural conservatives came supported a measure that reflected their small communities' patterns of commerce. Dolley claimed the law blocked hundreds of dubious ventures; the fees his office collected suggest a more modest scale of operation, and while the Banking Commissioner's office did shut down a Ponzi scheme and two dubious irrigation offerings, it could not prevent Kansans falling for a fake railroad promotion.

Keywords Blue Sky law · Kansas politics · Securities regulation · Fraud · Securities sales

Hit hard by his unexpected loss of his state House of Representatives seat in the 1910 election, under fire for underestimating the scale of the failed Abilene State Bank's cash shortage and still battling in courts to protect what he saw as his most significant political accomplishment, the reformed bank guaranty fund, Dolley started 1911 under a political cloud. Ousted from a legislature he had largely been able to run as Speaker of the House, he turned to a rival who had hinted before the November

D. Ress, *The Kansas Blue Sky Act of 1911*,
https://doi.org/10.1007/978-3-031-43831-8_4

1910 election that he might bid for the post, State Representative Cliff Matson of Wichita, "a progressive died in the wool," to collaborate on his political comeback. That would be a bill to regulate stock offerings—a bill that would not in the end, however, be enough to boost Dolley's hopes for a 1912 run for governor or to land Matson the Speakership he had sought. That post went to G. H Buckman, a former judge who had argued Dolley's case for the guaranty fund in the initial phases of bankers' challenges to the law.[1]

The Blue Sky Act was intended as "the outgrowth of an idea by Dolley put to work a year and a half ago," namely the Banking Commission's investment bureau.[2] He had decided that when Kansans wrote him asking about stock offerings, it longer was enough to tell them that "If there is a fake company among them I can pick it out and will do so and inform the investor of my opinion in plain words." Instead, he said, "All I want is that the Kansas farmer or workman who invests his money in any stock company gets a fair and square run for that money." After all, when the city slickers—"These men who sell stock are smooth as silk"—came to Kansas "They know every trick of their trade," Dolley said. "And they can make their schemes look as good as a government bond. They trick many shrewd and hard-headed farmers who know nothing of the wiles of the commercial world."[3] This was, it is important to note, not quite the same thing as pointing out a fraud. In world full of big dreams of new ventures—the companies that "may win … and again may not"—the plain talk of the busybody was not quite enough; and in a Kansas that "at this time is a fakir's paradise," even the shrewd farmer who could be bamboozled. Dolley's descriptions of the investment bureau's mission, however, would focus almost entirely on tales of widows suckered by obvious frauds. It was, after all, easier to swallow paternalism if the people protected were the most naïve: widows, for instance.

This was a rhetorical path he had followed before, when arguing for his bank guaranty fund after it was challenged in court. "Under the old way of doing things when the bank failed," he had said, the "mighty and the strong, who can afford to lose if necessary" would "walk out of the bank smiling as guaranteed depositors, receiving 100 cents on the dollar for their deposits. The farmer, the laboring man, the washwoman, and the widow were left to pay the loss," he told the *Topeka State Journal*.[4] "I will guarantee deposits if I have to sell the homes of every bank director of a failed bank and send them to the penitentiary to do it," Dolley said as drew up papers to force directors of one failing bank to sign over

$100,000 of property, to cover the deposits on the bank's books. "It was a hard job and only the threat of the penitentiary made some of the directors dig up the coin," the *State Journal*'s summary of Dolley's actions reported.[5]

Dolley's Blue Sky legislation was equally heavy handed. His law said companies and their sales agents hoping to offer stocks or bonds in Kansas had win permission to do so from him.[6] That permission depends not only on a determination that an offering was not fraudulent. Instead, the test was whether there was a good chance, in the Commissioner's opinion, that the buyer would make money. Dolley aimed at deals that disappointed expectations, not just fraud. Instead of after-the-sale lawsuits that disappointed buyers almost always lost, thanks to the caveat emptor rule, Dolley proposed to step between seller and buyer to prevent a purchase. No other government had tried anything like this. The only three that had by that time tried to regulate stock promotions—Connecticut, Nevada, and Rhode Island—had sought only to require companies file financial statements with state or county officials. In those states, the filing was all that was required. There was no requirement to distribute the financial statements to investors or for state officials to do anything if the information pointed to potential fraud. The three states' laws did not grant any authority to prohibit sales, even for companies that did not comply with the reporting requirement, and the Connecticut and short-lived Nevada laws only applied to mining companies.[7]

Dolley's bill, however, required companies file their business plans, copies of all contracts necessary to their business, physical copies of the securities proposed for sale, and a detailed report of financial condition. A company official had to certify, under penalty of perjury, that the information provided was accurate and correct. Investment banks and other dealers in stocks and bonds had to file regular reports on their financial condition as well as lists of the securities they were marketing as well.[8] The Kansas law went on to say that the Bank Commissioner could authorize sale of any shares or bonds only upon a finding that their filings showed they were solvent, that they had a "fair, just and equitable plan for the transaction of business" and that the securities promised a fair return to the Kansans buying them.[9] Review and follow-up investigation would be at the applicant's expense. If satisfied, the Commissioner would then issue a statement saying the company was authorized to sell its securities but with the warning in boldface type that he "in no wise recommends the securities to be offered."[10]

Once authorized to sell shares or bonds, a company had to file twice-yearly reports of financial condition, balance its books once a month, and allow stockholders, potential investors, and the Commissioner's staff to inspect its records.[11] It was a felony to "knowingly or willfully subscribe to or make or cause to be made false statements" or a false entry in a company's books intended to deceive examiners, and violators were subject a prison terms of up to ten years and fines of up to $10,000 (equivalent to more than $300,000 in 2023).[12] Only municipal bonds and securities issued by banks, building and loan societies, trust companies, and notes backed by mortgages on Kansas real estate were exempt. Bankers and elected officials, those rural grandees who were already trusted to manage savings and tax collections trust for their neighbors, were still to be at the center of Kansan finance and investments secured by Kansas land would be favored by law, reflecting Dolley's firm ideas that businesses ought to be financed locally. The exemptions, it is important to note, were for entities already regulated by the state—banks and trust companies by the Banking Commissioner, municipalities by the state legislature—while Kansas mortgage notes were secured by property and deeds of trust, with payment or seizure in lieu of payment enforced by courts. Dolley was inclined to protectionism—as indeed did the Progressive Party he would join in 1912, but there were practical justifications for the exemptions as well.[13]

Separately, the bill made investment bankers and other dealers in securities, whether based in Kansas or in any other state, subject to the same type of periodic examination that the Commissioner's office conducted on state banks. The cost of such examinations, including travel expenses, fell on the examined firm. If the Commissioner determined that a securities firm was insolvent, he could ask the state Attorney General to sue for a court order to place the firm into receivership.[14] Companies authorized to sell stocks and bonds, whether their own or on behalf of others were to display a copy of the state license in their offices and to give a copy to each canvasser to carry with him and display on demand from anyone solicited to buy securities. The Blue Sky Act also imposed criminal penalties, not just civil ones. It said selling unregistered securities was a misdemeanor and that anyone convicted of that could be jailed for up to 90 days and fined up to $5,000 (more than $150,000 currently).[15]

One matter Dolley said he would examine particularly closely was the level of commissions to be paid to stock salesmen and promoters, after finding that in some cases those amounted to thirty, forty, and even fifty percent of the sums Kansans paid for shares. He argued that any company paying high commissions to raise funds could not possibly be legitimate. While the Blue Sky law did not set a formal standard, Dolley told interviewers that he felt commissions should not exceed fifteen percent.[16] In short, Dolley's law said the state alone, through the Commissioner, should judge whether any share or stock would likely disappoint buyers or enrich the promoter unfairly, and that it could do so through an extraordinarily close look at the business of the company offering stock and the firms and agents actually making sales to individuals. What was at issue was not just fraud but the appropriateness of an offering.

In the Kansas House of Representatives, where Dolley was counting on allies from his days as Speaker, many of his fellow Republicans balked at his proposal. Criminal penalties and the power the legislation gave a single state official bothered them. They had, moreover, already shrugged off Governor Stubbs' complaints that his supposed Republican allies in the House were dawdling over all the most important items on the Progressive faction's agenda. House Speaker G. H. Buckman tried to strong-arm his caucus into voting for the Blue Sky legislation with a speech, unusual for the presiding officer, that "the state inspected banks, railroads and many other corporations and yet allowed hot air merchants and sellers of blue sky to come into the state in large numbers and sell worthless shares to Kansas people without restraint." State Representative F. S. Wettack objected, saying the bill "sought to substitute the brains of the bank department for the brains of the people." While Wettack said no members of the House objected to the idea of preventing wildcat mining and other highly speculative share offerings, "it was not necessary to make all corporations, whether they be mining, milling, brick, grocers, etc. go through an examination." State Representative Robert Stone, who had failed in a bid for the Speakership and who broke with Stubbs in a snit over an appointment to the state railroad board, also opposed the bill. Blue Sky law, they argued, was paternalism that would not wash in down-to-earth Kansas and that would burden hard-working Kansas business owners with necessary red tape.[17]

What support there was, was distinctly lukewarm. One supporter, State Representative Louis Schaumberg, a Democrat from western Kansas, complained that the bill "invests too much power in one person," even though "the bill will result in a great benefit to investors." Fellow Democrat and western Kansan M. B. Williams said he was willing to "chance the ills I know not off in this bill ...wishing to make it impossible for any man to secure…subscription to stock in any wildcat concern." Democratic State Representative J. M. Davis said he would reluctantly support the bill "Believing that this bill will in some measure protect the funds of the widows and others not possessed of sufficient information to properly invest their savings." Republican State Representative John Ostlind, another half-hearted supporter, said the bill "is probably covering too much space." But, he added, the biggest firm in central Kansas, a cooperative seed venture, said they would "invite inspection." With that reassurance, Ostlind said he would go ahead and vote for the bill because it "takes a shot at the fake companies." One Democrat, State Representative John Maloy, voted against the bill after saying he supported it since "regulating fake investment companies is necessary." Though both parties' floor leaders whipped the measure hard, many members broke with their party lines. Speaker Buckman and State Representative Matson rounded up 48 of 71 Republicans in favor; 16 of 53 Democrats ignored their whip to support Dolley's bill. The one independent, F. A. Hines of Scott City, voted against. The bill passed 63–52, with ten members not voting or absent.[18]

The bill passed the state Senate, where 35 of the 40 members were Republicans, with much less public fuss, although the *Topeka State Journal* reported in its only mention of the Senate action, two days after the vote, that "The blue sky bill found anything but pleasant sailing."[19] The state Senate Judiciary Committee recommended it nearly three weeks after the House passed the measure, with an amendment saying that any permits that the Banking Commissioner issued needed to carefully say he was not making a recommendation to buy the shares or bonds in questions.[20] The full Senate waited another two weeks before voting on the measure—according to the newspaper, only because of the scramble to round up support by state Senator Fred Quincy, a respected Progressive Republican, with a reputation for business acumen with his prosperous and bank.[21] The bill passed, with no reported debate, by a vote of 36 of the 40 state Senators. There were no votes against, with four Senators absent.[22]

The vote splits in the House suggest there may have been other factors than worries about paternalism and bureaucratic power at play. Not all Progressive Republicans, as was the case for Stone, supported regulation, nor did most Democrats, despite their Populist roots and basic hostility to financial interests. Stone's opposition, like the Democrats', clearly had more to do with their feelings about Stubbs. Tensions within the Republican House caucus threatened the bill, which would not have passed if Democrats had not broken ranks to vote for it, worried about the widows Dolley kept mentioning. It was, in the end, with those widows in mind that a reluctant state Senate went along with Dolley's bill. After the House vote, it seemed as if the fix was in. Even before the state Senate acted, Granite Securities Company published a notice in the *State Journal* advising "Legitimate Corporations" to contact it for its "plan of guarantee" to comply with the Blue Sky law when handling their stock offerings.[23] There was broad support for doing something about stock offerings, even (though perhaps only for image reasons) from at least some securities dealers.

Things moved quickly after the Blue Sky law was finally enacted. The day that Gov. Stubbs signed the Blue Sky bill into law, a dealer reportedly stopped by Dolley's office to ask how the law would affect the stock he had been selling. "I looked at his stock and found we had already investigated it thoroughly," Dolley said. It was, in his opinion, worthless, and:

> I told him he couldn't sell another dollar's worth in Kansas. He grew angry and said he guessed he could leave the state. I replied that the gates were open ... but that if he sold any more such stock he would find himself in the big state building over in Leavenworth... (where the state prison was located).[24]

Immediately with passage of the Blue Sky Act, "Dolley instructed his bank examiners, who are continually traveling about the state, to keep a lookout everywhere for 'investment agents'," the *Saturday Evening Post* reported.[25]

Dolley also asked the more than eight hundred state-chartered banks in Kansas to report any stock-peddling operations of which they might learn, telling them that "'If you hear of anybody offering any stock for sale ...find out whether he has a state license. If he hasn't, wire me and I will send an officer after him on the first train'," the *Post* added, noting that this was a particularly effective way of monitoring the stock boomers since

> Usually banks do hear of any stock-peddling operations that are going on in their localities, for the cash to pay for the stock comes out of a bank

> in one way or another. Naturally no banker likes to see money drawn out of his institution and put into a wildcat investment where neither he nor anybody else thereabout will ever see it again.[26]

There were, in Dolley's mind at least, hundreds of unsuitable stock promotions; in the first seven months after the Blue Sky Act took effect, he said he found just forty-five out of more than 500 applications reviewed offered a fair chance for Kansan investors.[27] His suspicions touched even the railroad, utility, and municipal bonds that Warren S. Hayden, an investment banker from Cleveland, showed him. Dolley told Hayden that each company or municipality on the list would need to submit detailed financial and operating information for review before the state banking commission would allow the securities to be sold.[28]

By May 1912, he was reporting that he had seen off more than seven hundred dubious investments and that he and his deputies had cleared fewer than one in ten applications to be offered in Kansas. Of the more than seven hundred others that he claimed he saw, the majority withdrew their applications when informed of how much information the Bank Commissioner's office demanded, or so he said.[29] In one case, after a review, he said he shut down the Kansas sales operation of a company that had thirty sales agents working, generating some $300,000 a month. All in all, Dolley claimed that 5,000 stock and bond salesmen "packed their grips and left the state" after the Blue Sky Act passed, estimated that they had taken Kansans for between $4 million and $6 million a year (he had previously in a speech at the Pleasant Ridge fair claimed to have saved Kansans $6 million within just six months).[30]

As for claims about the number of applications and approvals Dolley and his office processed, records of the fee payments that the Kansas Blue Sky Act required underwriters and actual issuers pay when applying for permits from the Banking Commissioner—$2.50 fee for each offering of shares of stock or bonds—show nothing close to those numbers ever crossed his desk. The filing fees collected for the fiscal year ended June 30, 1912, the first year the act was in effect, totaled $17.50—that is, a total of seven firms applied for permission to sell shares. Twenty-seven individuals had paid the $1 fee required for a dealer's license.[31] By September 30, 1912, the Bank Commissioner's office had collected fees from twenty-two more companies hoping to offer shares in Kansas; another forty-one individuals had applied for dealer's licenses and a total of forty-two companies had paid the $2.50 fee to accompany their first semi-annual financial report, a filing required to maintain a permit to offer shares in Kansas.[32]

Canadian Undersecretary of State Thomas Mulvey, a lawyer whose textbook *Dominion Company Law* would become a basic guide to Canadian corporate law, found some dubious deals still made it past Dolley's scrutiny in the first year of the Blue Sky Act's operation, though he provided few details about what he found in Dolley's files. The one instance he cited, an unnamed Chicago firm granted a temporary permit to raise $700,000 by selling shares in Kansas, declined to provide the financial reports state officials repeatedly demanded. By the time they ordered it to stop selling stock in Kansas, it had had enough time to raise that $700,000, Mulvey estimated. It went into liquidation within fifteen months, he said, and the Kansans who bought the shares suffered a total loss. Given Mulvey's failure to name the firm, it is hard to tell whether this, too, was another tale. There is no report of any such failure in Kansan newspapers, in any event.[33]

Dubious sales pitches continued, too. Even after the Blue Sky law took effect, promoters of the new Kansas Casualty and Surety Company still managed to pitch its shares with the typical get-rich-quick of a dubious deal: "100% Dividend. A Real Moneymaking Business," an even more grandiose (and unlikely) promise than Mr. Thompkins' had been. They could do this, moreover, while making asserting Kansans' investment was safe because "This Company operates under the Blue Sky Law."[34] The "Sure Profits For You," Kansas Casualty promised were backed by the self-contradicting claim that even before beginning business, it was making an annual income of $16,000.[35] By September 1912, the company said it sold a total of 50,000–60,000 shares to some 950 individuals, "including over 125 bankers and capitalists." The average investment was $287, well within the reach of the widows and small savers who critics of the Blue Sky laws would later insist were not the people who bought speculative securities Dolley tried to ban. Kansas Surety's first annual filing with the state insurance department showed how over-optimistic its approved pitch to investors was, for if all of its money after paying claims went to pay dividends—that is, if it had no office expenses and paid no salaries or agents' commissions—stockholders would have received a dividend of less than six percent. The company never came close to paying stockholders what it promised before shutting its doors after a disappointing 1921.[36]

The modest fee collections, the overheated claims of a Kansas Casualty, and the success Kansas promoter H. Leone Miller had with a promotion that Dolley banned make clear that the heavy hand that investment bankers feared seems not to have been quite as heavy as they feared. Despite the ban, Miller still netted $500,000 through an offering of shares in a notional railroad through central Kansas, linking Winnipeg, Manitoba, to the Gulf of Mexico. The money mainly came from bankers and well-to-do business owners in Kansas, Nebraska, and Oklahoma, "apparently immune to the much heralded 'blue sky' law of Kansas." Where things fell apart for Miller was in tiny Turon, Kansas, where he had made the unlikely promise to build a large forty-locomotive roundhouse as well as an ice plant and other facilities if residents committed just $2,500 to his railroad. The deal seemed especially odd to them (and in a way struck Dolley but that apparently did not strike the wealthy men and women who put money into the scam) after Miller claimed to have nearly $30 million on deposit in French banks; for it made them wonder why he would still need their $2,500.[37]

If Dolley did in fact reject (or simply discourage) hundreds of proposed offerings—neither he nor the Office of the Banking Commissioner saved any records of this—promoters of only three offerings made any traceable effort to reverse his rulings. The first were the backers of Sunny Kansas Sanitarium for Tuberculosis, which had received a temporary permit to sell shares, who complained to Governor Stubbs when Dolley shortly ordered it to stop selling shares "with no other explanation than that it did not seem to be a promising investment for the stockholders." The sanitarium was a new venture, having just erected its building five months before Dolley's order. It told Stubbs that if it had issued a dividend after completing the building, stockholders would have realized a twelve percent return on their investment. It did not mention the point, obvious to Dolley, that the only way to do that before patients arrived and began paying for their rooms would be draw the capital investors had already paid in. "If Mr. Dolley had not stopped us we could by now, no doubt, have been making considerable more," company Vice President E. E. Isenberger wrote, apparently conflating money received from selling stock as operating profits, a confusion that would have almost automatically convinced Dolley that Sunny Kansas was, in fact, nothing more than a scheme to fleece the public rather than a legitimate business. The sanitarium was, in fact, essentially a Ponzi scheme.[38]

Isenberger, like his two siblings and the brother of the company's treasurer, was a doctor and may not have clearly understood what Dolley considered financial viability. But one other indicator would later confirm for Dolley his sense that there was something off-kilter to the Bank Commissioner. Stubbs asked his secretary, Dave Leahy, to contact an old friend, W. B. Ham, who the Isenbergers said was a stockholder, for his views. "If they have something that is meritorious and fairly capitalized, the Governor thinks they ought to be allowed to sell stock in it," Leahy wrote. "If they have something that is pipe-dreamy and over-capitalized, the people of Kansas, at least, ought to be protected against it." Ham replied three days later that he "had never heard of the Sunny Kansas Sanitarium Company," that he had supposedly invested in and that while he had heard E. E. Isenberger (spelling the name Isenberg) was a good physician he had no personal knowledge about that.

Ham also noted the kind of concerns that bothered Dolley as he reviewed the Sunny Kansas records. On a recent trip, Ham wrote, "I saw from the car window at Natoma a rather pretentious building, some three fourths of a mile South of that town, and ... was told it was the Isenberg sanitarium." Hamm said he knew nothing about the property's value, about how many patients it had or what they paid or whether it was encumbered by a mortgage or other debts.[39] The sanitarium closed within a year, apparently after running into problems with a lack of water and several lawsuits; two years after Isenberger's complaint, it was torn down and its stones used to build a large home in Natoma.

At around the same time, the Rev. Festus Foster's brothers could not get their request to sell stock in the Louis Lake Conservation Company, a Wyoming irrigation scheme, past Dolley as quickly as they wanted. Fowler asked Governor Stubbs to step in and hurry his brothers' application along, since "there are several large investors waiting to come in, so that delay is working against us."[40] Checking, Stubbs's secretary Dave Leahy wrote to Foster saying Dolley "seems to think there is not enough financial responsibility back of the enterprise."[41] An old friend of Stubbs who also knew Foster tried to wave the pastor off: "I told him I didn't think Doctors or preachers knew much about such business propositions."[42] Foster persisted, writing directly to Stubbs to complain Dolley was pursuing grudge from when "My brother had been Mr. Dolley's pastor at Maple Hill and had had some controversy" over church finances. In addition, Dolley was on the school board and objected "when my brother's wife was teacher and Mr. Dolley's daughter was a student before the board for discipline."[43] Financing in Kansas—or in this case, a blocked deal—could still have a very small-town feel, it seems.

Foster told the governor in this letter that Dolley's own consulting engineer had found that the project was practical "from an engineering standpoint" but complained that the consultant's financial analysis ignored the principal asset of the project, some 40,000 acres of water, which the state of Wyoming valued at $50 an acre, as well as company's contractual commitment to build a power plant and water lines. Foster said he then gathered several written references attesting to the good character of his brothers and himself, and confronted Dolley's assistant, F. J. Patridge, who reportedly told him he was somewhat prejudiced "for there are so many damned preachers mixed up in finances that they know nothing about." When Foster went on to complain directly to Dolley, "he disclaimed any prejudice, but said 'the people of Kansas have been pouring money into irrigation for fifty years and have never got a dollar in return. If your company returns a dollar to Kansas investors in irrigate it will be the first company to do so.'"[44]

Stubbs' file on the matter includes a memo from Patridge which notes that the company had issued $1.51 million face value of shares but had actually received only $30,000 for these; the rest of the proceeds were simply IOUs. He noted that the offer for the power plant was not a firm contract and that Foster had not included the consulting engineer's comment that it would be "a physical impossibility to successfully finance this project with the remaining one hundred fifty thousand shares." The consultant had also concluded that the promoters would need to restructure their financing plan "on a more equitable and attractive basis" to secure the money actually needed to build the project, Patridge noted.[45] Even with this information Stubbs was not entirely sure he wanted to confront the pastor, so he asked Commissioner John T. White of the state Public Utilities Commission to look over the file and talk to the Fosters.

White agreed with Dolley's analysis that there was no tangible value to the company's assets—water rights and promissory notes for shares of stock it had managed to sell. "The people who buy this stock have no power in the company except to furnish the money and take changes on the prospective earnings," he concluded.[46] The irrigation project was, in short, an empty shell. Back in Wyoming, the company was issuing stock that would give holders a portion of its water rights to sweeten a parallel sale of land in a semi-arid region of the state. Its promotional fliers and mailings hinted that land then worth perhaps $10 or $20 an acre would rise in value to $100 once it built its water lines and would rise to as much as $1,000 an acre when cultivated.[47] It had nothing in hand to do what it said it would. While Dolley could be willing to let Kansans take on the risk of a Kansas Casualty and Surety Company, the irrigation project represented a degree of risk far larger, and perhaps almost as important, one that promised no real benefit to Kansas.

When a state investigation found Topeka land dealer Don A. Moun Day had been selling securities for a New Mexico land and irrigation scheme and a nearby sugar refinery without securing state approval but with prominent Kansas and Oklahoma politicians acting as fronts, Moun Day's lawyer complained that it was not fair to require business owners to put up significant sums of their own to launch an enterprise. He argued that Dolley's basic belief that many speculative offerings, though not necessarily frauds, simply did not have the resources to operate a mine or oil well, was unnecessarily fussy. It was too much power in the hands of one man, Moun Day's attorney argued. Kansas Attorney General John Shaw Dawson replied that the Blue Sky Act was a legitimate use of the state's police power, noting that the U.S. Supreme Court's rulings on challenges to Dolley's bank guaranty law had already confirmed Kansas's authority to intervene in financial dealings to protect it citizens.[48] The law, painted this way, was not paternalism—an overreach of state power to infringe liberty—but simply a way to address unfair dealings that current criminal law or civil lawsuits could not. Anyone who might eventually lose money with Moun Day's securities (a certainty given that Moun Day did not own any of the land or water rights at issue but only had options to buy them) would never be able to recover their money, for it would be long gone, Dawson argued. The Kansas Supreme Court agreed, taking less than a week to hand down its decision and appointing a receiver for Moun Day's companies at the same time.[49]

Dolley's law went beyond fraud—not to the point, as critics charged, of barring all risky but still legitimate business, as the permit for the struggling Kansas Casualty and Surety offering makes clear, but enough to bar the far more questionable promotions of Sunny Kansas Sanitarium and Louis Lake Conservation, as well as to clear the way for a court to stop Moun Day. So, for instance, when an Oklahoma promoter sought permission to sell shares in a company that claimed to have invented a new battery that would revolutionize booming electric power and machinery business, Dolley looked beyond the endorsements of prominent bankers and businessmen, and even a comment from a large railroad that it was testing the battery and that while it had were not yet completed its study "it looked like a marvelous thing to them." Unconvinced, Dolley asked the electrical engineering department at Kansas State University to take a look. After less than a month, they advised him that the battery did not work and Dolley barred the Oklahoman from selling stock in Kansas.[50]

Whether promising a new kind of battery, or sanatorium services, or irrigation of semi-arid lands, the offerings that Dolley rejected were from businesses that in his view simply should not have been financing themselves by selling shares. The backers of Sunny Kansas and Louis Lake had not put up enough of their own resources and the businesses had not yet started operating. On the other hand, while Kansas Casualty and Surety had not started selling insurance and surety bonds when it solicited the public, its founders had put up money and had arranged for the private placement of additional shares from their own network of well-off business owners and professionals. The distinction mattered. Putting up your own money or asking a trusted group to trust you to launch a business was a kind of financing Dolley would have been quite familiar with, going back to his early days as a grocer in Maple Hill when he bought into a neighbor's blacksmithing business. Kansas Casualty was an appropriate investment even though speculative and even with its inflated promises because its backers had put their own money in; promoters of the sanitorium and irrigation schemes had not: the difference was what made an offering a fair one with a sufficiently reasonable chance of profit for investors.[51]

Even the sharpest and most self-assured of those neighbors relied on that finding of appropriateness, as did the Kansas farmer that one national magazine highlighted in its report on the Blue Sky Act. In this tale, true or not, the farmer was enjoying the evening air on his porch and considering possibly using his $2,000 in savings to buy a car or some pastureland, the magazine reported, when a "brisk, breezy energetic" man stopped his car and strode up the driveway declaring that "the opportunity which poets say comes only once to a man in his lifetime is now knocking at your door." That opportunity, it turned out after many words of praise for the farmer's intelligence, was stock in an oil company, paying thirty percent now, fifty percent next year, and one hundred percent the year after that. "Have you a license to sell your stock?" the farmer asked, and the salesman, somewhat taken aback, said no because the company had only a few shares to sell in Kansas and only "wanted a few good people like yourself to get in on it." It was a classic pitch—a limited opportunity, little time to respond, and aimed at only a select few—by the farmer stood and said: "If you have no license you are wasting your time here."[52]

Notes

1. "Stubbs in the Race," *Topeka State Journal*, September 2, 1910: 1.
2. "Dolley's 'Blue Sky' Bill Is Ready to Be Signed," *Topeka Daily Capital*, March 8, 1911: 4.
3. "After The Fakirs," *Topeka State Journal*, April 8, 1910: 1.
4. "Favors His Case," *Topeka State Journal*, October 1, 1909: 1. J. R. Burrow, president of Topeka's Central National Bank had complained "If it had not been for the guaranty laws of Oklahoma (former state Bank Commissioner) Norton would have found it impossible to build up" the failed bank, adding that Oklahoma's guaranty fund had protected state government deposits totaling $464,504 which he said the bank's assets would have secured (he did not say anything about other depositors) "and in this manner the state watched its own accounts without any due regard to that of the stockholders." "As Seen Locally," Ibid., September 29, 1909: 7.
5. "Not a Cent of Cash," Ibid., February 25, 1910: 1.
6. Act of March 10, 1911, ch. 133, 1911 Kansas Session Laws, 210, sec. 12,3 at 210–211 (Blue Sky Act).
7. Louis Loss, *Securities Regulation*, Vol. 1 (Boston: Little Brown, 1951): 25–26.
8. Blue Sky Act, sec. 12,3 at 210–211.
9. Ibid., sec. 5 at 212–213.
10. Ibid., at 213.
11. Ibid., sec.s 8, 9, at 213–214.
12. Ibid., sec 12 at 215.
13. Ibid., sec. 1 at 210.
14. Ibid., sec.s 10 and 11, at 214–215.
15. Blue Sky Act, sec 13, at 216.
16. Marcosson, "Barring Out the Stock Thieves": 680.
17. "Goes With Rush," *Topeka State Journal*, February 8, 1911: 6; "Get Busy Says He," Ibid., February 9, 1911: 1.
18. Kansas House of Representatives, *House Journal*, 17th Biennial Session (Topeka: State Printing Office, 1911) 361.

19. "Stops the Train," *Topeka State Journal*, March 9, 1911: 8.
20. Kansas State Senate, *Senate Journal*, Seventeenth Biennial Session (Topeka: State Printing Office, 1911): 556.
21. "Stops the Train," Ibid., March 9, 1911: 8. William Connelly, *A Standard History of Kansas and Kansans*, Vol. 2 (Chicago: Lewis, 1918): 1880.
22. *Senate Journal*: 763.
23. "Legitimate Corporations," *Topeka State Journal*, March 1, 1911: 8.
24. "Dolly Told Him Gates Were Open for Him to Go," *Topeka Daily Capital*, March 18, 1911: 1.
25. Will Payne "How Kansas Drove Out a Den of Thieves, *Saturday Evening Post*, December 2, 1911: 71.
26. Ibid.
27. William R. Willcox, "The Average Man's Money," *Collier's*, October 28, 1911: 30 "The Kansas 'Blue Sky Law'," *Central Law Journal*, September 20, 1912: 222; "Promotion Schemes in Texas," *American Banker*, Vol. 77 (1912): 1386; Thomas Mulvey, "Blue Sky Law," *Canadian Law Times*, Vol. 36, No. 1 (January 1916): 38.
28. Proceedings of the Organization Meeting and of the First Annual Convention of the Investment Bankers' Association of America (Chicago: Investment Bankers Association, 1912): 139.
29. Joseph N. Dolley, "Blue Sky Law," *American Banker*, Vol. 77 (1912): 1705.
30. Joseph N. Dolley, "Biography of the Blue Sky Law," The Annalist, January 20, 1913: 11; "North Topeka News," *Topeka State Journal*, October 20, 1911: 12.
31. Records of the Office of Governor Walter Stubbs, Kansas State Archives, Topeka, Box 16, folder 4 item 2 Correspondence-State Departments: Accountant—Banking Commissioner audit.
32. Records of the Office of George Hodges, Kansas State Archives, Topeka. Box 18.6 Folder 10, item 6, Correspondence-State Departments: Accountant—Banking Commissioner audit.
33. Mulvey, "Blue Sky Law," 39.
34. "100% Dividend," *Topeka State Journal*, January 9, 1913: 3.
35. "Sure Profits for You," *Topeka State Journal*, May 18, 1912: 3; "100% Dividend," Ibid., January 9, 1913: 3 "Another 100% Dividend By A Surety Company," Ibid., January 23, 1913: 3.

36. "Strong Endorsements of a Strong Institution By Strong Men," *Topeka State Journal*, September 9, 1912: 6; "100% Dividend," Ibid., January 9, 1913: 3; Annual Report of the Superintendent of Insurance of the State of Kansas for the Year Ending December 31, 1913 (Topeka: State Printer, 1914): 63; Annual Report of the Superintendent ... 1914: 64; Annual Report of the Superintendent ... 1918: 68; Annual Report of the Superintendent ... 1921: 68, 110. For the view that speculative investments did not target small savers see, e.g., Jonathan R. Macey & Geoffrey P. Miller, "Origin of the Blue Sky Laws," *Texas Law Review*, Vol. 70, no. 2 (December 1991): 390–391.
37. "Kansas Railroad Vision Vanished" *Abilene (Kansas) Weekly Reflector*, October 10, 1912: 12. Miller tried to overcome Turon residents' doubts by hiring a surveyor to map a route between Salina and the town, but stiffed the surveyor, who went to court; the court-appointed receiver found the railroad's assets amounted to $800, mostly office furniture. "Paper Railroad Sold for $800," *The Beaver (Oklahoma) Herald*, December 5, 1912: 1. Miller reacted to the mail fraud charge by firing off profanity-filled letters to a Salina lawyer and a stenographer who had worked for him that brought the Post Office back to him with new charges of sending obscene material through the mail. He served eighteen months for that charge, while the mail fraud case did not proceed. "Miller Found Guilty," *Topeka State Journal*, November 27, 1913: 3; "Won 158 Cases," Ibid., July 11, 1914: 7.
38. E.E. Isenberger to Walter Stubbs, March 25, 1912, Records of the Office of Governor Walter Stubbs, Kansas State Archives, Topeka, "Correspondence-State Departments," Box 17, folder 6, item 31.
39. Dave Leahy to W.B. Ham, May 4, 1912; W.B. Ham to Walter Stubbs, May 7, 1912. Records of the Office of Governor Walter Stubbs, Kansas State Archives, Topeka, "Correspondence-State Departments," Box 17, folder 6, item 31; "Osborne County Hall of Fame Honors," https://ochfhonors.wordpress.com/2021/10/29/honors-in-architecture-notable-structures-of-farm-and-home-in-osborne-county-kansas-part-one/.
40. Festus Foster to Dave Leahy, April 6, 1912; Records of the Office of Governor Walter Stubbs, Kansas State Archives, Topeka, "Correspondence-State Departments," Box 17, folder 6, item 32.
41. Leahy to Foster, April 9, 1912, Ibid.

42. Charles Sumner to Walter Stubbs, undated, Ibid.
43. Foster to Stubbs, July 6, 1912, Ibid.
44. Ibid.
45. F.J. Patridge memorandum, undated, Ibid.
46. John H. White to Walter Stubbs, August 12, 1912, Ibid.
47. "15 Reasons Why," Ibid.
48. "No State Worry," Topeka State Journal, June 24, 1913: 1; "Dolly Is Sued," Ibid., July 2, 1913: 1; Don A. MounDay and Wife Arrested Today," Ibid., July 25, 1913: 1, 6; "The Blue Sky Law," Ibid., August 8, 1913: 1; "MounDay Loses," Ibid., August 11, 1913: 1; "Both Are Guilty," Ibid., January 20, 1914: 1, 6.
49. "MounDay Loses," Ibid., August 11, 1913: 1.
50. "The Kansas 'Blue Sky Law," *Central Law Journal*, September 20, 1912: 222.
51. Dolly, "Biography of the Blue Sky Law," *The Annalist*, January 20, 1913: 11.
52. Marcosson, "Barring Out the Stock Thieves": 674.

Bibliography

Act of March 10, 1911, ch. 133, 1911 Kansas Session Laws, 210 (The Blue Sky Act).

Annual Report of the Superintendent of Insurance of the State of Kansas, 1913, 1914, 1918, 1921.

Records of the Office of George Hodges, Kansas State Archives, Topeka. Box 18.6, Correspondence-State Departments: Accountant—Banking Commissioner audit.

Records of the Office of Governor Walter Stubbs, Kansas State Archives, Topeka, Box 16, Correspondence-State Departments: Accountant—Banking Commissioner audit and, "Correspondence-State Departments," Box 17.

Anonymous. 1909a. "As Seen Locally," *Topeka State Journal*, September 29: 7.

———.1909b. "Favors His Case," *Topeka State Journal*, October 1: 1.

———. 1910a. "Not a Cent of Cash," *Topeka State Journal*, February 25: 1.

———. 1910b. "After the Fakirs," *Topeka State Journal*, April 8: 1.

———. 1910c. "Stubbs in the Race," *Topeka State Journal*, September 2: 1.

———. 1911a. Goes with Rush," *Topeka State Journal*, February 8: 6.

———. 1911b. "Get Busy Says He," *Topeka State Journal*, February 9: 1.

———. 1911c. "Legitimate Corporations," *Topeka State Journal*, March 1: 8.

———. 1911d. "Dolley's 'Blue Sky' Bill Is Ready to Be Signed," *Topeka Daily Capital*, March 8: 4.
———. 1911e. "Stops the Train," *Topeka State Journal*, March: 8.
———. 1911f. "Dolly Told Him Gates Were Open for Him to Go," *Topeka Daily Capital*, March 18: 1.
———. 1912a. "Sure Profits for You," *Topeka State Journal*, May 18: 3.
———. 1912b. "Strong Endorsements of a Strong Institution By Strong Men," *Topeka State Journal*, September 9: 6.
———. 1912c. "The Kansas 'Blue Sky Law'," *Central Law Journal*, September 20: 222.
———. 1912d. "Promotion Schemes in Texas," *American Banker*, 77: 1386.
———. 1912e. "Kansas Railroad Vision Vanished," *Abilene (Kansas) Weekly Reflector*, October 10: 12.
———. 1912f. "Paper Railroad Sold for $800," *The Beaver (Oklahoma) Herald*, December 5: 1.
———. 1913a. "100% Dividend," *Topeka State Journal*, January 9: 3.
———. 1913b. "Another 100% Dividend by a Surety Company," *Topeka State Journal*, January 23: 3.
———. 1913c. "No State Worry," *Topeka State Journal*, June 24: 1.
———. 1913d. "Dolly Is Sued," *Topeka State Journal*, July 2: 1.
———. 1913e. "Don A. MounDay and Wife Arrested Today," *Topeka State Journal*, July 25: 1, 6.
———. 1913f. "The Blue Sky Law," *Topeka State Journal*, August 8: 1.
———. 1913g. "MounDay Loses," *Topeka State Journal*, August 11: 1.
———. 1913h. "Miller Found Guilty," *Topeka State Journal*, November 27:3.
———. 1914a. "Both Are Guilty," *Topeka State Journal*, January 20: 1, 6.
———. 1914b. "Won 158 Cases," *Topeka State Journal*, July 11: 7.
Dolley, Joseph N. 1912. "Blue Sky Law," *American Banker*, 77: 1705.
———. 1913. "Biography of the Blue Sky Law," *The Annalist*, January 20: 11.
Investment Bankers Association. 1912. *Proceedings of the Organization Meeting and of the First Annual Convention of the Investment Bankers' Association of America* (Chicago: Investment Bankers Association).
Kansas House of Representatives. 1911. *House Journal, 17th Biennial Session*. Topeka: State Printing Office.
Kansas State Senate. 1911. *Senate Journal*, Seventeenth Biennial Session Topeka: State Printing Office.
Loss, Louis. 1951. *Securities Regulation*. Boston: Little Brown, 1951.
Macey, Jonathan & Geoffrey P. Miller. 1991. "Origin of the Blue Sky Laws," *Texas Law Review*, 70: 348–397.
Marcosson, Isaac. 1912. "Barring Out the Stock Thieves," *Munsey's Magazine*, February: 674–680.
Mulvey, Thomas. 1916. "Blue Sky Law," *Canadian Law Times*, 36: 38.

Payne, Will. 1911. "How Kansas Drove Out a Den of Thieves," *Saturday Evening Post*, December 2: 3–5.
Willcox, William R. 1911. "The Average Man's Money," *Collier's*, October 28: 30.

CHAPTER 5

Accepting Regulatory Paternalism: A Wise Man to Look Out for You

Abstract Kansas Banking Commissioner Joseph N. Dolley's Blue Sky Act addressed Americans' deepening distrust of the stock promotions that came with increasing frequency in the first decades of the twentieth century. Although financial writers tried to address this, urging readers to turn to bankers and lawyers for advice, legislators in other states hastened to enact laws that followed the Kansas model with state officials stepping in to vet offerings for appropriateness.

Keywords Paternalism · Investment banking · Securities regulation · Stockbrokers

The idea that people generally could not look out for themselves when buying stocks or bonds was, in fact, commonly accepted at this time. It was how stockbrokers and financial writers sold their services to a public still generally unfamiliar with corporate securities. This helped make Dolley's Blue Sky Act approach seem a legitimate exercise of state power in a nation ordinarily quite jealous of any supposed infringement on liberty of action. Dolley's tales of apocryphal widows duped by hordes of sweet-talking stock salesmen also reinforced that impression of general incompetence in finance, for they played so directly to common perceptions of the day, stereotypes about women and their remoteness from

D. Ress, *The Kansas Blue Sky Act of 1911*,
https://doi.org/10.1007/978-3-031-43831-8_5

the hurly-burly of business. It was, in his stories as well as those financial writers made up, natural for women to turn to someone else, always a man experienced in the ways of the world, to look out for their interests. As the stockbroker Fred Rollins comfortingly suggested in his pamphlet "A Financial Courtship," the paternalism of such a man was women's best protection. In Rollins' tale, when a long-time court clerk died and left his 42- and 32-year-old unmarried daughters a life insurance benefit of $50,000, the innocents wondered what to do. "Oh, I know, the magazines are full of things," the younger daughter said:

> Here's one; just listen: '100 per cent, profit; send us $100 and in six months we guarantee to return you your money and $100 additional.' Just think of that! Why, we could put in the whole $50,000 and double our money ... Here's another: The K. T. Oil Company — 300 per cent, profits; no risk; stock in $10 shares. Send for prospectus.'" "Well, it seems easy enough to invest, doesn't it?"

Her wiser, older sister fretted that they also often read of bunco schemes: "How is one to know?" she wondered.[1] One could know, as matters turned out in this tale, by turning to a wiser, older counselor. A family friend directed them to a lawyer who volunteered to give them lessons in finance, beginning with a lesson about money that made the fictional sisters' lack of knowledge seem quite childlike. After several lessons, interspersed with the younger daughter's piano recitals, came a warning from the lawyer about investing in stock. "Perhaps it sounds more dangerous than it is, but I never advise women to buy stocks anyway," he said. For women, he continued, the safest course was to invest in the highest quality bonds or mortgages, even if the return seemed modest. In the end, he proposed marriage to the younger daughter and helped shepherd the two women's money into a diversified mix of bonds, a mortgage note and savings accounts at two different banks.[2] Though this fictional lawyer was the hero in a tale told by a stockbroker, and like a brave knight in a fairy tale, ended up marrying his princess, the point of the story was that the view he shared with Dolley: stocks—even the most gilt-edged—were inappropriate for many individuals.

The idea that shares of stock might not be appropriate ways to save for some individuals, and that they might not be appropriate means to finance some enterprises, is the essential concept underlying the Blue Sky Act. It is, however, easy to overlook, in part because of the style of Dolley's tale-telling and in part because the idea of inappropriateness is not commonly part of economic analyses that hold that markets—including capital markets—inevitably find the best interests of millions of actors. The scissor-like Demand and Supply curves that the great British economist Alfred Marshall sketched in his leading textbook of the day remain a potent metaphor, even though Marshall also warned of "the absence of any adequate knowledge of the business on the part of the shareholders who undertake its chief risks."[3] Only much later would Yale University's Irving Fisher become perhaps the first prominent economist to suggest shares might be "most desirable form of investment" for everyone, though he also warned that there was little governments could to protect investors from the exaggerated financial claims of stock promoters.[4]

In the tales Dolley and the financial writers told, those widows and hapless stenographers, schoolteachers, and modest maidens needed someone to look out for them. The supposed wise men were at the center of stories about stock swindles because, with what at the time was a generally unquestioned view of women's vulnerability and poor judgment, they drove home the underlying paternalistic message of both Dolley's Blue Sky law and the investment bankers' bids to be trusted. So, too, was the wise elder necessary when others ventured to deploy their savings: "For the young investor to attempt to select safe securities without some outside honest and experienced aid, is a great mistake," as the popular investment counselor Roger Babson wrote in his first guidebook for the public.[5] For Dolley, like Babson and the brokers and the banks, it was necessary to stress that the wise counselor, whether a banker and regulator like Dolley or a bond and stock dealer like Rollins, needed to step in to protect the innocent.

$300,000,000 IS OUR NATION'S ANNUAL TRIBUTE TO GET-RICH-QUICK SHARKS

J. N. DOLLEY of KANSAS

AND TELL THEM KANSAS IS ALL RIGHT

J. N. Dolley, of Kansas, peerless investigator of get-rich-quick schemes, says the people of this country are swindled out of $300,000,000 every year by so-called investment companies. Dolley is bank commissioner in Kansas. In the last year he has routed some 500 stock salesmen out of his home state. The legislature gave his department control over investment agents and companies, and when six hundred of these made application for licenses to do business, Dolley had them looked up and allowed licenses in just forty-seven cases.

"There are more Rufus Wallingfords within two blocks of Times Square, New York, now," he says, "than you can find in all of Wichita. You just tell the public that Kansas is all right."

It is from the Rock Island Argus, a *Defunct Daily Newspaper*, December 30, 1910

Dolley broadcast that message widely. Articles boasting about his successes defending Kansans—usually widows—against con men selling shares reached national audiences in *Saturday Evening Post*, which declared "The Blue Sky Act, in short, is a real law with real teeth in it,"[6] as well as *Colliers, World's Work, Munsey's, Current Literature*, and *Metropolitan Magazine*. Dolley did not stop with that, either, for he sought to reassure bankers and investors in their specialist journals, though with little success. Wire services and news feature syndicates told newspaper readers that "Fake Stock Sellers Run out of Kansas" and that "many fake promoters...like the Arab 'folded their tents and silently stole away'"—even as far as Canada to escape the fate of one Utah promoter "now languishing in jail."[7]

In one editorial cartoon-centered newspaper feature, Dolley reassured readers that "There are more Rufus Wallingford within two blocks of Times Square New York ... than you can find in all of Wichita. You can just tell the public that Kansas is all right," referring to the character from George Randolph Chester's lighthearted tales of the modern Yankee peddler who tricked foolish rich men into buying his blue sky shares.[8] Big city sophisticates took notice. *The Washington Times*, echoing the oft-repeated and gendered naïf versus trickster tales Dolley favored, reported that "Widows, especially new widows with a little insurance, were among the most fruitful prospects" for the "financial vultures" who Dolley targeted. "Kansas has found a way to eliminate the sharks," the financial columnist of *The Detroit Times* told readers. Massachusetts' former Bank Commissioner, Arthur B. Chapin, declared that "While it may seem unnecessary interference for the state to attempt to dictate what persons shall do with their money ... bait of large dividends or visions of wealth" had lured too many who could not afford the loss into wildcat mining and oil promotions. And Dolley summed it up in another syndicated article: "It has been said that the people do not need a guardian to supervise their investments, but I want to say to you, and the most of you will agree with me, that a large per cent of them do need a guardian, especially in matters of this kind."[9]

Dolley read the language of the Kansas Blue Act broadly. "Here is the case of a corporation with a high-sounding title, duly incorporated under the laws of a sovereign state," he told one reporter, as he described how his suspicions were raised by the company letterhead showing it operated out of offices in Chicago, 1,000 miles away from where it was incorporated. It was, of course, fairly common for companies to be based far from the states, such as New Jersey or Maine, that had wooed incorporation fees by enacted laws giving corporations sweeping powers, cutting short the otherwise highly political process of moving a charter embodying similar powers through a state legislature.

Dolley, however, shrugged this off. "A beautifully typewritten letter from the president, on fine linen paper, sets forth that the company is engaged in developing and marketing a tract of one hundred and twenty-five thousand acres of fruit land in Central America specially adapted to banana culture," Dolley continued. In this version of the Pan-American Plantations come-on, the letter described how the company was in line to receive title to the land once it paid $2.50 an acre, although its marketing material aimed to excite potential buyers about their likely windfall by telling them that similar land is already selling for $20 an acre. This made no sense to Dolley. When Dolley asked for more information, the company sent Dolley's office "a handsomely engraved stock certificate on bond paper that looks quite like a Government bond" as well as reports on the land and a list of "a quite imposing list of directors," Dolley said, adding:

> All this looks very plausible. One trouble with it is, it looks too plausible. Why should gentlemen who can buy land for two dollars and a half an acre and very soon sell it for twenty dollars be coming out to Kansas in order to raise the necessary capital ... incidentally paying a large commission to stock-peddling agents?

So, Dolley (or, more likely, an assistant) investigated. He did not uncover anything particularly alarming about the promoters and the investigation found:

> The land is undoubtedly there, and from the best information obtainable it seems to be very good land, quite suitable for fruit culture and capable, under proper management, of returning good profits.

But Dolley kept checking, inquiring with the government that supposedly signed the land sales contract. With this step, he learned that the government had repudiated the deal. His suspicions that something was awry finally confirmed Dolley then refused to allow the stock sale.[10] This was no casual or quick review, in other words. The investigation involved checks of court records and business reputations of individuals far from

Kansas, as well as of the distant, undeveloped land in Central America. It also meant international contact with a government to check on the status of a contract for an option on land. And it all started with the smallest of matters: a rural banker's suspicion of what had become a standard practice of incorporating a business in a state with easygoing law while operating in another.

Another rejected offering was for a railroad promising to carry enormous volumes of traffic from a still undeveloped territory. "I cannot tell how many ciphers there are in the capitalization; but ... The corporation doesn't pretend it has any railroad now," Dolley said. As he asked about the men listed as directors on the company's letterhead, he learned that one individual, "though he doesn't figure so prominently on the letterheads as some others, is really the guiding spirit." Checking into the unnamed individual's background, Dolley found he jumped a $60 bail bond, and before that had defaulted on a small loan. His questions sparked several letters from bankers, including one, far from Kansas, recalling a transaction from four years before, who wrote that "All the common honesty" in the promoter's character "could be put in the hull of a mustard seed."[11] Inquiries that reached to central American governments' land offices or creditors stiffed in distant states were not the kind of research that Fisher or Selden or Rollins or dozens of other investment handbooks of the day suggested. They had a different tale to tell.

Dolley's small-town views on how to finance business, and how not to, were still commonly held and were reflected in the rush of approving comments in other states, as well as hasty moves in many to regulate securities sales. "Every year financial schemes which are either downright fakes or at least so questionable in character that no person of training in financial affairs would investment in them, cost the plain people of this country hundreds of millions of dollars," an Arizona editor commented shortly before the first session of Arizona's new state legislature met and passed a copy of Dolley's law.[12] Launching his third party bid for the presidency in 1912, Theodore Roosevelt said he would sign federal legislation that like Kansas would ensure "an absolute control" over offerings of stocks and bonds to the public, although he subsequently dropped this promise while campaigning. He would still later rebuff the notion altogether: paternalism would have only a fairly short-lived fad in the land of liberty.[13]

In rural backwaters, enthusiasm for Blue Sky laws was strong: "Nebraska has been a gold mine for these sharks...the blue sky law is an honest measure for the protection of innocent people and no legitimate business proposition will suffer because of it," a Farmers' Congress official said.[14] "The sale of stocks and bond in Indiana by crooked promoters will be prohibited ... hundreds of thousands of dollars will be kept in legitimate channels," an Indiana editor chimed in.[15] Iowa State Representative Frank Shane promised voters in 1912 that if they re-elected him, he would introduce the Kansas Blue Sky law in Iowa, where stock boomers "promising large and extravagant dividends ... frequently succeeded in making the sale, and the widow or orphan who had thus unwisely invested their money were fleeced out of the entire amount."[16] The Blue Sky law, by barring any offering "found to be unstable"—not merely fraudulent—"has done away with the swindling of millions of dollars in the state of Kansas and will do the same for Iowa people," an Iowa weekly editor wrote.[17] The target of Blue Sky law, a West Virginia editor wrote, was "some glib agent" promising promised ten to twenty percent dividends that "are usually 'will-o-the-wisps'." These "tempt one to the edge of the precipice and over he goes, money, faith, happiness and all," the editor continued, concluding that the Kansas Blue Sky Act was "a very good law."[18]

When Vermont State Representative J.C. Flynn proposed a Kansas model law in that state, his fellow legislators, promising an end to "the mulcting of Vermonters by companies which gave alluring promises of splendid returns," stood up for small-town commerce and a tradition of self-reliance. The people the legislators sought to protect were not only the gullible and easily duped, either, as *The Barre Daily Times* commented. "The losers were not always dullards in business" since some were more than competent with ordinary transactions like the store credit, loans, and shareholdings in the small businesses of Vermont. It was not possible for even a sharpest farmer or small-town business owner to look over the actual operation of a distant company or inspect its books, as they would have with a local proposition "as a result of which many were fleeced."[19] Acting, then "to prevent unscrupulous agents and investment companies from working off worthless securities in the state," Vermont adopted the Kansas law in 1912 with the addition of a review and licensing requirement for sales of land outside the state and a ban on advertising unlicensed securities. The target in Vermont, as in Kansas, was not only outright fraud, but the "sale of securities and western lands to gullible persons whose cupidity is aroused by glittering tales of financial success" since "Possibly not all of these securities are utterly worthless, but in the main they are sold, even those that have some value, at much more than they are worth," the Bennington *Evening Banner* commented, apparently not minding the potential loss of advertising revenue.[20]

Although mining interests fought Blue Sky initiatives aggressively, a weekly newspaper editor in South Dakota's mining hub argued that "A vast sum has already been saved to the small investors in Kansas by this law, and a similar saving will result in South Dakota....The people are entitled to this protection."[21] For some business leaders, the real victims when "Mr. Sucker" fell for "Mr. Faker's" promise of thirty percent annual dividends from a fictional gold mine were legitimate miners and legitimate financings, when the investor puts up money for development and the prospector a mineral claim so "if we succeed we will all make our thousands ... if we fail, we must all sail in the same ill-fated vessel," as one California mining journal argued.[22] In California, home to many of the oil company stocks Dolley particularly objected to, Chester H. Rowell, a newspaper editor from Fresno, convinced fellow Republican progressives to enact the Kansas law, but with additional provisions that also "would make it tough sledding for the installment sharks and the loan sharks."[23]

Within two years, eleven states and the Province of Manitoba enacted their own Blue Sky laws, modeled on the Kansas statute's ban of not only fraudulent offerings but also those that were found to be unfair to investors. Another nine states enacted narrower laws allowing the ban of offerings state officials deemed to be fraudulent. Arizona, Arkansas, California, Idaho, Michigan, Montana, North Dakota, Ohio, South Dakota, Tennessee, and West Virginia generally followed the Kansas model by allowing regulators to forbid sales of securities if they determined the terms were unfair to buyers, although California's law specifically limited oversight to initial offerings only.[24] Florida, Georgia, Iowa, Missouri, Nebraska, North Carolina, Oregon, Texas, and Wisconsin declined to give state officials to power to bar the sale of securities if they felt the shares or bonds would not offer a fair return, although they could bar offerings when officials' reviews determined a proposed deal to be fraudulent.[25]

In Arizona, the first state to follow Kansas, the State Corporation Commission cracked down after Southwestern Oil and Development pitched itself to investors by saying the then-pending Blue Sky Law would govern its offering. The company said it was developing shale oil fields in the state and to do that would sell one million shares, with a par value of $1, at a deep discount of 10 cents each. That was exactly the kind of discount that Chicago Board of Trade investigator John Hill had long since warned was a sign of a dubious investment. Like some of the Kansas Casualty and Surety advertisements, Southwestern Oil's marketing claimed that the success of other, similar businesses assured its own promises of gains for holders of its shares, since "Arizona Oil May Make as Many Millions for Stockholders as California Oil Has Done."[26] Arizona never did become much of an oil patch, and when the Arizona Blue Sky Act took effect, one of the Corporation Commission's first acts was to suspend Southwestern's offering for violating the act.[27]

For, while "The perennial foolishness of people who lose their money in these wildcat schemes would seem to possess elements of humor," as the *Metropolitan Magazine* noted, the cost was devastating to people who had little, like a Pennsylvania widow (living in a state that would for many years to come decline to enact a Blue Sky law) with nine children who put all her $200 savings into a stock promoted by the infamous Franklin Everhart, and wrote asking for help as she was penniless and faced losing her home, or a South Carolina carpenter (in another non-Blue Sky law state) who put a $900 insurance award, paid after losing his hand, into another Everhart promotion. Everhart was a New York promoter whose frauds included wheat deals that promised weekly dividends of three percent (that is, a 177% return on principal over a year) and the Index Mining Co, which netted him more than $2 million before a Post Office fraud order barred those promotions from the mails.[28] That order didn't stop him: his U.S. Cereal promotion, promising weekly dividends of two percent, took in more than $1 million in just a few months.[29]

It seemed that there were always some people who could not resist the promises of large, regular dividends from the sure things the various Mr. Thompkins had on offer. "A man doesn't have to be so very smart to see the ear-marks of a graft which sells a stock cheap and promises unheard of returns at the end of six months," one North Dakota editor sighed. "But it is exactly for that line of buncombe that many fall, and to save whom it was necessary to pass the Blue Sky Law." Nevertheless, it was unlikely to help much, the editor argued, for in a time of wonders—airplanes, radios, multi-million-dollar stock market fortunes:

> The trouble is there are so many engaged in following the fakes in an effort to hand over their hard earned money. People may not believe in witches, or madstones, or electric belts as much as they used to, but there are so many new kinds that they can usually find something to follow.[30]

Notes

1. Frank W. Rollins, *A Financial Courtship, or A Plea for Conservative Investments* (Boston: N. Sawyer, 1906): 9.
2. Ibid., 35–36, 63, 65, 68.
3. Alfred Marshall, *Principles of Economics* (London: Macmillan and Co., 1890): 365.
4. Irving Fisher et al. *How To Invest When Prices Are Rising* (Scranton, PA: G. L. Sumner & Company, 1912): 144; *The Nature of Capital and Income* (New York: Macmillan, 1906): 74–75, 78, 80.
5. Roger Babson, *Bonds and Stocks: The Elements of Successful Investing* (Wellesley Hills, MA: Babson's Statistical Organization Inc. 1913): 15.
6. Will Payne, "How Kansas Drove Out a Den of Thieves," *Saturday Evening Post*, December 2, 1911: 71.
7. "Fake Stock Sellers Run out of Kansas," *Waxahachie (Texas) Daily Light*, September 26, 1911: 3; "Kansas Blue Sky Law," *Omaha (Nebraska) Bee*, October 12, 1911: 4.
8. All that was needed for a blue sky promotion, the fictional Wallingford told his follow con-man Blackie Daw, was to "bait up with some little staple….See this swell red carpet fastened down with rusty tacks? There's the chance. Suppose those tacks were covered with red cloth to match the carpet. Blackie, that's my next invention." So was born the Eureka Carpet Tack company. The company would pay "sixteen per cent. a year dividends," Wallingford told one investor, adding "within two months after we had started our factory wheels rolling we could sell out to the Eureka Company for two million dollars; or a profit of more than one thousand per cent." George Randolph Chester, *Get-Rich-Quick Wallingford, A Cheerful Account of the Rise and Fall of an American Business Buccaneer* (New York: A.L. Burt, 1908): 18, 26.
9. "A good thing from the state of Kansas," *Washington Times*, December 21, 1911: 10; "Advice to Investors," *Detroit Times*, November 14, 1911: 9; Chapin's comments were reprinted in "The Blue Sky Law," *Fergus County Democrat* (Lewiston, Montana) October 22, 1912: 2; Dolley's in "Blue Sky Law of Kansas," *The True Democrat* (Bayou Sara, Louisiana), September 7, 1912: 2.

10. Will Payne "How Kansas Drove out a Den of Thieves," *Saturday Evening Post*, December 2, 1911: 71.
11. Ibid.
12. "Kansas 'Blue Sky' Law," *Bisbee (Arizona) Daily Review*, October 26, 1911: 3.
13. "Roosevelt Taunts Wilson About Tariff," *New York Sun*, September 3, 1912: 4; Theodore Roosevelt, *Theodore Roosevelt, an Autobiography* (New York: Charles Scribner's Sons,1922): 160.
14. "O'Dell Defends The Blue Sky Law," *Omaha Daily Bee*, August 16, 1914: 6c.
15. "A New Basic Law for the State Asked," *Richmond (Indiana) Palladium and Sun-Telegram*, January 10, 1913: 8.
16. "Representative Frank Shane Goes On Record in Favor of 'Blue Sky Law'," *Ottumwa (Iowa) Tri-weekly Courier*, October 22, 1912: 4.
17. "Good for Iowa," *Audubon County Journal* (Exira, Iowa) January 9, 1913: 1.
18. "Wild Investments," *The Daily Telegram* (Clarksburg, West Virginia) February 23, 1912: 4.
19. "Protecting Vermont Interests," *The Barre (Vermont) Daily Times*, February 15, 1913: 4.
20. "A 'Blue Sky' Bill," *The Bennington (Vermont) Evening Banner*, November 13, 1912: 2.
21. "A Blue Sky Law," *Custer (South Dakota) Weekly Chronicle*, June 22, 1912: 1.
22. Editorial (No Headline), *Los Angeles (California) Mining Review*, June 8, 1912: 5.
23. "Discord Rends State Moosers," *The Call* (San Francisco), September 24, 1912: 1, 3.
24. Act of May 18, 1912, ch. 69, 1912 Arizona Session Laws at 338; Arkansas Securities Act, No. 214, § 6, 1913 Arkansas Acts at 904; Investment Companies Act, ch. 353; 1913 California Statutes at 71;.Idaho Securities Act, ch. 117, 1913 Idaho Session Laws at 454; Act of May 2, 1913, No. 143, 1913 Michigan Public Acts at 243; Act of March 13, 1913, ch. 85, § 9, 1913 Montana Laws at 367; Supervision of Investment Companies, ch. 109, 1913 North Dakota Laws at 137; Act of Apr. 28, 1913, § 16, 1913 Ohio Laws 743; Act of March 14, 1913, ch. 319, 1913 South Dakota. Laws at 522; Act of September 27, 1913, ch. 31, 1913 Tennessee Public

Acts at 500; Act of February 6, 1913, ch. 15, 1913 West Virginia Acts at 114. Manitoba's law was Sale of Shares Act, 1913,2 Geo. 5, ch. 75.

25. Act of May 20, 1913, 1913 Florida. Laws ch. 6422; Act of August 19, 1913, No. 263, 1913 Georgia. Laws 117; Act of April 19, 1913, ch. 137, 1913 Iowa Laws at 137; Act of April 7, 1913, 1913 Missouri. Laws at 112; Act of April 21, 1913, ch. 199, 1913 Nebraska Laws at 603; Act of March 12, 1913, ch. 156, 1913 North Carolina Session Laws at 249; Act of February 281,913, ch. 341, Oregon General Laws at 688; Act of August 21, 1913, 33d Legislature, ch. 32, 1913 Texas General Laws 66; Act of August 21, 1913, ch. 756, 1913 Wisconsin Laws at 1108.
26. "Oil in Arizona," *Arizona Republic* (Phoenix, Arizona), January 12, 1913: 18.
27. "Operation of the Blue Sky Law in Arizona," *The Copper Era and Morenci Leader* (Clifton, Arizona) August 8, 1913: 2.
28. Karl Decker, "Easy Money, the Story of the Get-Rich-Quick Graft," *The Metropolitan Magazine*, March 1911: 701, 704.
29. "Alleged Swindler Caught," Washington Herald, September 1, 1910: 1.
30. "Following The Fakes," *The Evening Times* (Grand Forks, North Dakota) September 12, 1911: 2.

Bibliography

Act of May 18, 1912, ch. 69, 1912 Arizona Session Laws.
Act of February 6, 1913, ch. 15, 1913 West Virginia Acts at 114.
Act of February 28, 1913, ch. 341, Oregon General Laws at 688.
Act of March 12, 1913, ch. 156, 1913 North Carolina Session Laws at 249.
Act of March 13, 1913, ch. 85, § 9, 1913 Montana Laws at 367.
Act of March 14, 1913, ch. 319, 1913 South Dakota. Laws at 522.
Act of April 7, 1913, 1913 Missouri. Laws at 112.
Act of April 19, 1913, ch. 137, 1913 Iowa Laws at 137.
Act of April 21, 1913, ch. 199, 1913 Nebraska Laws at 603.
Act of April 28, 1913, § 16, 1913 Ohio Laws 743.
Act of May 2, 1913, No. 143, 1913 Michigan Public Acts at 243.
Act of May 20, 1913, 1913 Florida. Laws ch. 6422.
Act of August 19, 1913, No. 263, 1913 Georgia. Laws 117.
Act of August 21, 1913, 33d Legislature, ch. 32, 1913 Texas General Laws 66.

Act of August 21, 1913, ch. 756, 1913 Wisconsin Laws at 1108.
Act of September 27, 1913, ch. 31, 1913 Tennessee Public Acts at 500.
Arkansas Securities Act, No. 214, § 6, 1913 Arkansas Acts at 904.
Idaho Securities Act, ch. 117, 1913 Idaho Session Laws at 454.
Investment Companies Act, ch. 353; 1913 California Statutes at 71.
Sale of Shares Act, 1913, 2 Geo. 5, ch. 75 (Manitoba).
Supervision of Investment Companies, ch. 109, 1913 North Dakota Laws at 137.
Anonymous. 1911a. "Fake Stock Sellers Run out of Kansas," *Waxahachie (Texas) Daily Light*, September 26: 3.
———. 1911b "Kansas Blue Sky Law," *Omaha (Nebraska) Bee*, October 12: 4.
———. 1911c. "Advice to Investors," *Detroit Times*, November 14:9.
———. 1911d. "A Good Thing from the State of Kansas," *Washington Times*, December 21:10.
———. 1912a. "Wild Investments," *The Daily Telegram* (Clarksburg, West Virginia) February 23:4.
———. 1912b Editorial (no headline), *Los Angeles (California) Mining Review*, June 8: 5.
———. 1912c "A Blue Sky Law," *Custer (South Dakota) Weekly Chronicle*, June 22: 1.
———. 1912d. "Roosevelt Taunts Wilson About Tariff," *New York Sun*, September 3:4.
———. 1912e "Discord Rends State Moosers," *The Call* (San Francisco), September 24: 1,3.
———. 1912f. "Representative Frank Shane Goes On Record In Favor Of 'Blue Sky Law'," *Ottumwa (Iowa) Tri-weekly Courier*, October 22: 4.
———. 1912g "A 'Blue Sky' Bill," *The Bennington (Vermont) Evening Banner*, November 13:2.
———. 1913a. "Good for Iowa," *Audubon County Journal* (Exira, Iowa) January 9 1913: 1.
———. 1913b. "A New Basic Law for the State Asked," *Richmond (Indiana) Palladium and Sun-Telegram*, January 10: 8.
———. 1913c. "Protecting Vermont Interests," *The Barre (Vermont) Daily Times*, February15: 4.
———. 1914. "O'Dell Defends The Blue Sky Law," *Omaha Daily Bee*, August 16: 6c.
Babson, Roger. 1913. *Bonds and Stocks: The Elements of Successful Investing* (Wellesley Hills, MA: Babson's Statistical Organization.
Decker, Karl. 1911. "Easy Money, the Story of the Get-Rich-Quick Graft," *The Metropolitan Magazine*, March: 701–704.
Fisher, Irving. 1906. *The Nature of Capital and Income*. New York: Macmillan.

———. 1912. *How to Invest When Prices Are Rising*. Scranton, PA: G. L. Sumner & Company.

Marshall, Alfred. 1890. *Principles of Economics*. London: Macmillan and Co.

Payne, Will. 1911 "How Kansas Drove out a Den of Thieves," *Saturday Evening Post*, December 2:3–5.

Rollins, Frank W. 1906. *A Financial Courtship, or A Plea for Conservative Investments* Boston: N. Sawyer.

Roosevelt, Theodore. 1911 *Theodore Roosevelt, an Autobiography*. New York: Charles Scribner's Sons.

CHAPTER 6

Rejecting Regulation as Paternalism: The Busybody's Heavy Hand

Abstract As more states adopted Kansas Banking Commissioner Joseph N. Dolley's Blue Sky Act to regulate securities sales, brokers specializing in mining shares, soon joined by the larger Wall Street and regional investment banks, began publicity and lobbying campaigns charging the law was a paternalistic infringement on American liberty. Their first efforts, however, had mixed success.

Keywords Blue Sky law · Caveat emptor · Commerce clause · U.S. Constitution · Securities law

Willard Done, Utah's Insurance Commissioner, returned to Salt Lake City from the National Association of Insurance Commissioners' annual convention in the summer of 1912 with the news that regulators in other states were planning to introduce versions of Utah's groundbreaking law setting standards for fraternal insurance. Those small life insurance policies issued by burial societies or lodges or associations like the Modern Woodmen or the Sokol societies or Knights of Columbus were like the one that Mr. Thompkins knew meant there was money to be had when he talked the widow into investing in Pan-American Plantations. Commissioner Done also had a shopping list of good ideas from his colleagues for the Utah state legislature: a bill calling for standardized

D. Ress, *The Kansas Blue Sky Act of 1911*,
https://doi.org/10.1007/978-3-031-43831-8_6

requirements for accident and health insurance policies, a measure to make it easier to convict embezzlers, another banning "parlor" or white phosphorous matches, a fire hazard because a sunbeam could set them alight and because their ignited heads often broke apart when struck and, still-burning, flew into flammable paper or cloth. On his list from the convention, too, was the Kansas Blue Sky Act.

It was aimed, Done said, at "insurance grafters" who sold shares in fraudulent new companies, and the name, he explained, "originated in the saying 'long green for blue sky'." For several years by then, insurance regulators had run across the worthless securities scam—it was a natural enough outgrowth of a business that did a lot of its marketing (and handled a lot of its collections) door to door, as well as a business where many mutual companies sold whole life insurance policies, which included a savings component creating a cash value that was supposed to grow over time. These policies conflated the idea of ownership—a mutual insurer is formally owned by its policyholders—with investment, exactly as the traditional view of buying a stock did for Dolley when he bought stock in a telephone company, a flour mill, and the Stockgrowers State Bank. A widely read insurance trade journal's report on the door-to-door salesman's pitch that Pennsylvania farmer William Sampson fell for—to cash in one paid-up policy for a fraction of its ultimate cash value to buy a junk policy that included an option to buy shares in a corporate shell—made clear that buyers rarely understood what they were buying. The report also suggested why Done might have been one of the very few insurance commissioners to urge a Blue Sky Act: the actuary for the junk policy and shares Sampson bought also worked for Pennsylvania's insurance regulator, for connections between the companies and their regulators were in many states uncomfortably close.[1]

In most states that considered enacting a Blue Sky law, the impetus came from a banking commissioner, public utilities commission, or state legislators. Unlike those officials, however, Commissioner Done would have little luck convincing legislators in Utah, home of a busy market in mining shares, and a place where dreams of buried wealth resonated strongly within a religious community whose central scriptures were revealed in just that way. The Utah legislature briskly rejected a Kansas modeled securities law, cheered on by Utah editorialists and the influential mining industry, complaining of a paternalistic overreach that would freeze future development of the state's resources. The claim that Blue

Sky laws were paternalism and that they infringed liberty derailed Dolley's movement.

> "At the best, the law says to the investor 'You have not sense enough to know what to do with your money,'" Galen Norris, a Kansan "standpatter" Republican opponent of Dolley and Stubbs, told Utahans: adding that if they want to "exercise their own right as American citizens to use their money as they see fit, they will oppose any such law."[2] The law "practically prohibits the sale of any stock ... it would sound the death knell of mining," a Salt Lake City stockbroker somewhat frantically claimed, while colleagues added that it would give a state official (in Utah's case, despite Done's role introducing the bill, this was to be the bank commissioner, exactly as in Kansas) "complete and arbitrary power ... practically nothing but the momentary condition of his stomach being a guide as to his favorable or unfavorable action."[3] Another comment played on local pride, for "it is notorious that eastern people, who may be expected to have similar feelings to bank commissioner ... are almost without exception, united in condemnation of mining industries, A hostile atmosphere is thus introduced at the start."[4]

Dismissing complaints that mining promotions fleeced the gullible, as Utah's legislature began considering its own Blue Sky act, one weekly sniped:

> one thing is lacking to make the operation of the proposed 'blue sky' law a grand, sweet song, and that is the investors to be protected. Maybe the Bank Inspector can find them. The brokers have been looking for them without success.[5]

A week later, it elaborated that:

> Those who are ignorant of financial affairs usually cling to the belief that there is a way, if only it can be found, to double capital three or four times a year without incurring risk of loss ... the innocent investor in blue sky either wants more than he has a right to expect for his money ... the legislature might pass a law forbidding an investor to make a hog of himself.[6]

With hints of the effete easterner or ill-informed banker interfering with the independent westerner's knowledge and inclination to take a risk, a focal point of opposition to Blue Sky law was the idea accepting that a single person—a busybody—could say anything about, a central element of western identity. "Whew! What a power reposed in one man! Where is a man big enough, competent enough and honest enough in whom to repose such a power," one Utah editor commented.[7] Power, too, that would be exercised out of sight and arbitrarily; power that could act mistakenly, just as the gossiping busybody, with the sly hints and whisperings of so many tales would.

To cast a state official as a busybody, that self-appointed guardian of community interest, might in fact do more harm than good tapped into an unsettling concern for many. This was the unease reflected, for instance, in Horatio Alger's story about one youth's career had been temporarily derailed when a "gossip and busybody mistook" the youth's tin box for one that went missing from the local bank.[8] A deeply unpopular character, "The busybody is a self-appointed inspector of social warts ...He can live on anything; he usually carries with him a bag of reputations made up in cold hash so he doesn't have to stop for meals," the Reverend Madison C. Peters declared in column widely reprinted in western newspapers.[9] So, even as Theodore Roosevelt tentatively toyed with the idea of a national Blue Sky Act if he defeated President William Howard Taft in the 1912 election, Taft told a New Jersey rally: "I do claim that it is evidence that I have not made a busybody of myself and interfered with the natural laws of trade and prosperity."[10] In the end, Roosevelt backed off his Blue Sky Act pledge.

The argument that Dolley's Blue Sky law was an overbearing interference with an intelligent citizenry's ability to look after its own interests worked effectively in some states. Despite the Massachusetts state legislature's resolution for a study to consider state regulation of stock offerings, a resolution passed just days after Gov. Stubbs signed the Kansas act into law, a state study commission dismissed the Kansas model as unnecessary and probably unconstitutional.[11] The study commission reported that it had seen no complaints about the way that bankers and brokers, the usual sellers of stocks and bonds in the state, handled these transactions. "It is also not intended to go too far in the line of paternalism or in making the Commonwealth an insurer of the investments of its private citizens," the commission report concluded.[12]

In New York, after the Assembly—the lower house—approved a Kansas model bill, Wall Street mobilized to kill the measure in the state Senate, cheered on by the Republican stalwarts of the *New York Tribune,* which argued that the "foolish 'blue sky' law" would "compel investors to choose between the devil and the deep blue sea."[13] On Wall Street, the consensus was that the paternalism of a modified Blue Sky law "may be alright for Kansas," as one banker put it, "but it would mean the dire entanglement of the business of the country" if enacted in New York, creating "possibilities of almost unlimited graft upon corporations" (though what such graft might look like the banker did not say).[14]

The Blue Sky Act was "Paternalism run mad," the *United States Investor* charged, and it was "open to objection as savoring too much of paternalism," the somewhat more restrained critique of *Investments* magazine.[15] The Kansas law fell on one side of the "opposing principles of paternalism and democracy ... by passing in advance on the merits of concrete transactions," Cleveland banker Warren Hayden told the organizational meeting of the Investment Bankers Association, which formed mainly in response to Dolley's law and the growing interest other state legislatures had shown in it. "Those who hold to one view think it is part of the business of the state to consider in advance the merits of concrete transactions," he said. "Those who have the other view think that the business of the state is to inflict penalties for transgressions of a prescribed general rule."[16]

Opponents of other proposals to regulate or restrict businesses had found little success when charging paternalism, a tactic adopted even before Dolley's Blue Sky law initiative. Insurance executive J.S. Rowe argued without success against workers' compensation law "with its stamp of paternalism," insisting that a system aimed at paying for treatment of workplace injuries would lead to "a complete abandonment of individualism," but states hastened to adopt the approach as a way of limiting businesses' exposure to potentially costly lawsuits.[17] New Jersey Congressman James Hamill failed, too, when he opposed a pension proposal for government employees by calling it "paternalistic hand of the government."[18] Oregon got deputies for the state forester and several fire wardens even as the state capital daily newspaper complained the move was "nothing but the extension of socialistic functions and professional paternalism that battens armies of officials on the ordinary citizen."[19] Wisconsin's proposed state-run life insurance fund looked like "paternalism, nothing else" to some, but it nevertheless was set up (and still exists).[20] Irrigating land and selling it ought to be left to private land companies, a Nevada editor declared, but "Settlers .... believing in the great paternalistic idea have sought the government's new irrigation projects for a solution of the home owning question." Irrigation came.[21]

Americans laughed at some of more extreme complaints of paternalism, or shrug off what were in fact paternalistic interventions into daily life. Governments "with paternalistic solicitude for passengers and employees" required railroads to install safety devices," grumbled a New Mexican railroad executive, but they went up nevertheless despite "enormous cost to the railways."[22] Virginians drank bourbon even though "Prohibition is a cardinal dogma of the paternalistic theory," one Richmonder noted in a letter to the editor of his daily newspaper.[23] With such reactions in mind, perhaps, the editors of the *Harvard Law Review*, asking if legislation should protect "the ignorant and improvident from loss in the stocks or securities of 'wild-cat' schemes of a fraudulent or highly uncertain nature," found it easy to conclude that there was "a strong public interest in the general freedom of business and the liberty of the individual to buy and sell as he chooses."[24] Yet the public by and large did not rally to the cause of reining in supposed paternalism: people liked railroad level crossing guards and signals, it seemed.

Still, investment bankers thought they had powerful case to make against regulation by tagging Dolley's Blue Sky Act as paternalism—and, moreover, as ill-informed paternalism that understood less about the realities of investment than did a new audience of intelligent, independent-minded middle-class Americans who the bankers were beginning to target in their marketing. Investment Bankers Association general counsel Robert Reed wrote that "a general law regulating necessary business transactions cannot be based on the assumption of incompetence of persons legally competent to manage their affairs" and concluded that "It is quite evident from the language used that the original draftsman [of Kansas model Blue Sky regulation] ... knew nothing of the normal investment security business."[25] John Hogan, a financial advisor who said he directed people to potentially lucrative shares, said Blue Sky laws had emerged from "the private sanctums of the entrenched money sharks" and the "holier than thou bunch" who were "foisting upon the public an enormous quantity of bonds, many of which are showing losses to investors." Paternalism and the moralizing busybody kept the investing public "from exercising its free will to select and purchase speculative issues."[26]For Alan G. Hoyt, a banker who served as chair of the Investment Bankers Association's legislative committee, "'Blue Sky' laws are but a manifestation of a tendency in our political development which is fraught with great danger ...the paternalistic idea of regulation by commission or public officer or perhaps by direct legislative enactment of almost every sphere of business activity."[27] Louis Guenther, editor of the *Financial World*, which boasted of the many investment scams it exposed and declared its aim was to look out for the best interests of the less knowledgeable, said states should not try to say "what investors should or should not put their money into," for "We are not a nation of fools, as these laws seem to imply."[28]

Even in Medicine Lodge, Kansas, stung by railroad bond disappointments and with business owners among the many gulled by George Brinkman and James Armstrong's vending machine stock scam, paternalism could seem a potent argument. As the community's weekly newspaper asked: "when an omnipresent, powerful protecting influence watched over" individuals "Would not the man so treated as a child soon become thoughtless and improvident as a child?"[29] His was, however, not a common view in the small communities of the rural mid-continent. Editors across the Plains states published, with evident approval, a story about the paternalism of a New York grocer who, perhaps like the grocers in their own small communities (even, maybe, Dolley in the day), told a child asking for the two pounds of sugar his mother wanted, to take only one "and go kind of slow on that." In this little morality tale, the New Yorker explained, to the approval of the editors and presumably their readers, "that is the only way on earth to keep those people from running into debt."[30] In Utah, one editor commented that "In these days of 'blue sky' laws for everybody," the state ought to consider adopting an Iowa town's truth-in-advertising requirement for itinerant merchants with "fire sale" or "bankruptcy sale" goods on offer.[31]

Paternalism, in short, could be a tricky concept to pin down. Freedom might mean one thing to an investment banker—the freedom to strike a deal—but it might mean something different to mother in a New York slum or a Kansas farmer: the freedom that comes when you have not run out of money because of a thoughtless or improvident purchase. Despite all the dire warnings about paternalism, West Virginia's elected State Auditor John Sherman Darst could defend his state's Kansas model law with little personal political consequence, declaring:

> public sentiment had not been sufficiently aroused to overcome the opposition of the unscrupulous professional promoters who adopting as their motto that good old legal phrase—'Caveat emptor'—Let the buyer beware, and parading the bogey paternalism … had no conscience as to methods, so long as they could defeat such legislation.[32]

Eventually, even New Yorkers skeptical of Dolley's approach saw a need for some government action to oversee stock offerings. "In general the tendencies of our government are not paternalistic," the *New York Tribune* wrote, adding:

> But the need of some parental restraint on the readiness of Americans to send remittances to almost anybody who can ...issue a temptingly baited investment prospectus is painfully evident....it generally turns out when some mining concern which has never sunk a shaft or located a claim is run to ground in luxurious offices...that the bulk of the purchasers of its securities are people of fairly good education and moderate means—often professors, teachers and other professional men ...Tens of thousands of Americans seem to think that the only thing which stands between them and wealth is some great financial opportunity soon to appear around the corner.[33]

Dolley was typically blunt. "Apparently some of the people engaged in it think they have an inalienable constitutional right to sell worthless 'securities'; and they resent any interference with their operations as an act of tyranny and oppression," he told one magazine writer. Soon after the Kansas act took effect, "two well-dressed, prosperous-looking gentlemen" called on him to say they "were surprised and rather indignant" because Dolley had "peremptorily rejected" a stock they were interested in selling. "They thought the commissioner must be mistaken as to the sort of gentlemen he was dealing with; they had good clothes, jewelry and money in the bank; were well acquainted with various substantial and more or less leading citizens," Dolley's tale went. When they had finished their pitch, Dolley asked: "How long have you been selling stocks round here?" "Seven years," they replied. "You must have sold stocks in that time to a good many people," the Commissioner innocently asked. "Oh, yes; a great many," came the reply. "Good!" Dolley fired back. "I'll give you two dollars a head for all the people you will bring to my desk who ever bought stock of any kind from you and got back as much as five per cent of their money!" At that point, Dolley concluded, the two promoters hastened away.[34]

Notes

1. "The victim of a Eureka Life Stock Selling Scheme," *Life Insurance Independent*, Vol. XX, No. 3 (March 1908): 63. William

Sampson, a Washington County, Pennsylvania farmer, had cashed in a legitimate, $25,000 life insurance policy and paid a hefty $617 premium for a Eureka policy including the right to buy Eureka shares at $20 each, when the market price was $25 after insurance agent Lee Hepler told him future dividends would cover future premium payments. Six months later, Hepler returned, with a special offer for more shares at $25 when they were about to go to $30. Sampson bought twenty more shares. A week later, Hepler returned, saying there was a chance to round out Sampson's holding with at the $25 per share price for another one hundred eighty shares, for $4,500. In the end, Sampson paid $7,000 for shares in a company that was not authorized to sell insurance in Pennsylvania—so his policy was as worthless as shares in a company that had issued $427,000 worth of coverage, backed by a reserve of just $1,537.

2. "Blue Sky Law Not Popular," *Salt Lake Tribune*, March 26, 1913: 10.
3. "Blue Sky Law Has Stirred Brokers," *Salt Lake Tribune*, February 21, 1913: 12.
4. "Blue Sky Laws," *The Logan (Utah) Republican*, March 25, 1913 p. 4.
5. "Mining and Financial," *Goodwin's Weekly* (Salt Lake City, Utah), March 1, 1913: 7.
6. "Mining and Financial," *Ibid.*, March 8, 1913: 7.
7. "Not In Love With New Blue Sky Law," *The Evening Standard* (Ogden, Utah), February 26, 1913: 10.
8. Horatio Alger, *Struggling Upward or Luke Larkin's Luck* (New York: Hurst & Co., 1900) 66-76.
9. "Meddling Men," *The Raymer Enterprise* (Weld County, Colorado), September 14, 1911: 7.
10. "Now Up To Voters," *Evening Star* (Washington, D.C), May 28, 1912: 10.
11. "Resolve to Provide for an Investigation," *Acts and Resolves Passed by the General Court, 1911* (Boston: Secretary of the Commonwealth, 1911) 1058–1059; Commonwealth of Massachusetts state Senate, Senate Report No. 167 (January 1913), cited in C.A. Dykstra "Blue Sky Legislation," *The American Political Science Review*, Vol. 7, No. 2 (May, 1913): 233.
12. Massachusetts Senate Report No. 167.

13. "See Graft in Blue Sky Law," *The New York Sun,* March 27 1913: 9; Untitled editorial comment, *New York Tribune*, March 28, 1913: 8.
14. "See Graft in Blue Sky Law," 9.
15. "Unwise Security Legislation" *United States Investor*, February 24, 1912: 312' "Some Things The Prospective Stockholder Should Know," *Investments*, Vol. V, No. 4 (April 1912): 139.
16. Proceedings of the Organization Meeting and of the First Annual Convention of the Investment Bankers' Association of America (Chicago: Investment Bankers Association, 1912) 139, 141, 145–147.
17. J.S. Rowe, "Workmen's Compensation Insurance," *The Market World and Chronicle*, January 28, 1911: 6.
18. "Favor Hamill Bill," *Washington Evening Star*, January 19, 1912: 1.
19. "Only Another Hundred Thousand," *Daily Capital Journal* (Salem, Oregon), January 9, 1911: 2.
20. "Paternalism, Pure And Simple," *Washington (D.C) Herald*, (October 29 1912): 4.
21. "Amendments Needed," *The Churchill County Standard* (Fallon, Nevada), August 14, 1912: 2.
22. "The Trespass Evil On American Railroads," *Albuquerque (New Mexico) Morning Journal*, December 8, 1912: 6.
23. "Prohibition" (letter to the editor) *Richmond (Virginia) Times-Dispatch*, December 24, 1911: 4.
24. "State Regulation of the Sale of Stocks, Bonds, and Other Investment Securities" *Harvard Law Review*, Vol. 27, No. 8 (June, 1914): 742.
25. Robert Reed, "Blue Sky Laws," Annals of the American Academy of Political and Social Sciences (March 1920): 179, 187.
26. John Hogan to (Illinois securities division Chicago office director) Arthur. G. Davis, May 3 1923, cited in Daniel Holt, Acceptable Risk: Law, Regulation and the Politics of American Financial Markets 1878–1930, PhD dissertation, University of Virginia, 2008.
27. "A Surfeit Of Bad Laws," *Financial World*, November 8, 1913: 20.
28. "Why Not A Federal Blue Sky Law," *Ibid.*: 10.

29. "Fatal To Progress," *Barber County Index* (Medicine Lodge, Kansas), February 9, 1910: 3.
30. "Paternalism In Groceries," *Bismarck (North Dakota) Daily Tribune*, January 20, 1911: 6.
31. Editorial (no headline) *Eastern Utah Advocate* (Price, Utah), March 27, 1913: 4.
32. "Blue Sky," *The Daily Telegram* (Clarksburg, West Virginia), (November 19 1913): 2.
33. "Easy Marks," New York Tribune, January 23, 1912: 6.
34. Will Payne "How Kansas Drove out a Den of Thieves, *Saturday Evening Post*, December 2, 1911: 71.

Bibliography

Alger, Horatio. 1900. *Struggling Upward or Luke Larkin's Luck* New York: Hurst & Co.

Anonymous. 1908. "The victim of a Eureka Life Stock Selling Scheme," *Life Insurance Independent:* March 1908: 63

———. 1911a. "Only Another Hundred Thousand," *Daily Capital Journal* (Salem, Oregon) January 9: 2

———. 1911b. "Prohibition" (letter to the editor) *Richmond (Virginia) Times-Dispatch*, December 24: 4

———. 1912a "Unwise Security Legislation" *United States Investor*, February 24: 312

———. 1912b "Some Things The Prospective Stockholder Should Know," *Investments*, V: 139

———. 1912c. "Amendments Needed," *The Churchill County Standard* (Fallon, Nevada) August 14: 2

———. 1912c: "Paternalism, Pure And Simple," *Washington (D.C) Herald*, October 29: 4

———. 1912d: "The Trespass Evil On American Railroads," *Albuquerque (New Mexico) Morning Journal*, December 8: 6

———. 1913a. "Blue Sky Law Has Stirred Brokers," *Salt Lake Tribune*, February 21: 12

———. 1913b. "Not In Love With New Blue Sky Law," *The Evening Standard* (Ogden, Utah) February 26: 1

———. 1913c. "Mining and Financial," *Goodwin's Weekly* (Salt Lake City, Utah) March 1: 7

———. 1913d. "Mining and Financial," *Goodwin's Weekly*, March 8: 7

———. 1913e. "Blue Sky Laws," *The Logan (Utah) Republican* March 25: 4

———. 1913f. "Blue Sky Law Not Popular," *Salt Lake Tribune*, March 26: 10.
———. 1913g. "See Graft in Blue Sky Law," *The New York Sun*, March 27: 9.
———. 1913h "Why Not A Federal Blue Sky Law," and "A Surfeit Of Bad Laws," *Financial World*, November 8: 10, 20
———. 1914. "State Regulation of the Sale of Stocks, Bonds, and Other Investment Securities" *Harvard Law Review*, 27: 742
Commonwealth of Massachusetts. 1911 *Acts and Resolves Passed by the General Court, 1911*
———. 1913. Senate Report No. 167
Dykstra, C.A. "Blue Sky Legislation," *The American Political Science Review*, 7: 232–233
Holt, Daniel. 2008 "Acceptable Risk: Law, Regulation and the Politics of American Financial Markets 1878–1930," PhD dissertation, University of Virginia.
Investment Bankers Association, 1912. *Proceedings of the Organization Meeting and of the First Annual Convention of the Investment Bankers' Association of America* Chicago: Investment Bankers Association
Payne, Will, 1911 "How Kansas Drove out a Den of Thieves, *Saturday Evening Post*, December 2: 3–5
Reed, Robert. 1920. "Blue Sky Laws," *Annals of the American Academy of Political and Social Sciences* March: 179–187.
Rowe, J.S. 1911. "Workmen's Compensation Insurance," *The Market World and Chronicle*, January 28: 6

CHAPTER 7

Court Challenges to Regulation: The Judges Step In

Abstract Investment bankers had only limited success with their publicity and lobbying efforts against the Blue Sky Act. But they quickly turned to challenge Kansas model laws, but not the Kansas law itself, in court. Federal trial courts in Michigan, Ohio, Iowa, and West Virginia found merit in the bankers' arguments that the Blue Sky Acts of those states were an unconstitutional interference with interstate commerce. Some found as well that the laws granted too much power to a single official and that the laws treated in-state firms differently from out-of-state firms, another violation of the Constitution. State courts, including Kansan courts, did not tend to rule this way and when moderately revised Michigan and Ohio laws came before the U.S. Supreme Court, the justices upheld them as legitimate exercises of police power.

Keywords Blue Sky law · Caveat emptor · Commerce clause · U.S. Constitution · Securities law

It probably did not help either Dolley or the main opponents of his Blue Sky Act as they bid for public support that they all were bankers: "All the banker stories I know have a Kansas setting" as one later folklorist noted. "The Kansas farmer's folk-idea of the banker is that of an annoyingly indispensable fellow," this scholar added.[1] Even the ideal

D. Ress, *The Kansas Blue Sky Act of 1911*,
https://doi.org/10.1007/978-3-031-43831-8_7

banker was hardly an empathetic figure, for the banker was "In business ... a firm believer in and rigid enforcer," Iowa's State Librarian, Johnson Brigham, commented. This wise counselor might be "firm but kind – not indulgent," he continued, but bankers were "too true to well-grounded, time-tested business principles to be swerved ... by tearful pleas for the suspension of inexorable rules."[2] "Just look at'em!" said George Amberson Minafer to the young woman he was courting in Booth Tarkington's novel *The Magnificent Ambersons*, as they watched wealthy couples dancing at a ball. "Lawyers, bankers, politicians! ... What do they ever know about real things?" Where do they ever get?".[3]

Dolley, in the event, did not get the political success in Kansas that he had hoped for, never reaching the turreted red-brick governor's mansion at Eighth and Buchanan streets in Topeka. After his hopes to become governor of Kansas fizzled, he lost his chairmanship of the Republican Party and then failed to win a state Senate seat. Nor was he particularly successful in winning support from the small-town bankers he was supposedly fronting for in proposing the Blue Sky Act. Though he believed, along with many Kansan bankers, that "there is a determination and policy among western men to do their financiering themselves," his clashes with them over the interest they could charge, the people who could hold their stock, and the guaranty fund assessments and administration won him few friends, and they were happy to see him ousted as Banking Commissioner after the 1912 election, when Democrat George H. Hodges edged out Dolley's friend and business associate Arthur Capper by twenty-nine votes statewide—an election Hodges eked out with the support of "regular" Republicans opposed to Stubbs, Capper, and Dolley.[4]

Dolley's opponents in the Investment Bankers Association, on the other hand, also had little political luck with their campaign against the Blue Sky Act. In their case, the argument that the law was excess of paternalism had the same limited effect as it had for others in debates over prohibition, workers' compensation, and state foresters. Securities dealing firms had known for some time they faced a challenge from Dolley's Blue Sky Act. But as legislatures in other states shrugged off their paternalism argument, investment bankers quickly tried to mute that growing movement by saying a degree—a minimal degree—of regulation might be a good idea. "Our danger is not that we would be embarrassed by the operation of well-conceived blue sky legislation, but rather that the legislation may be brought forward by those who have no familiarity with the financial mechanism of the country," Cleveland investment banker Warren Hayden argued. The problem, he argued, with regulation was with the Kansas model that said that "it is part of the business of the state to consider in advance the merits of concrete transactions."[5] Hayden, instead, suggested an alternative role for the state: "First, licenses; second, publicity; third, penalties."

> We would have every one who may offer securities in the state affected required, first, to obtain a license from the proper banking officer. We would not have the license depend upon the applicant's means, but upon his character and his standing,

while "Of course the great mass of applicants could be passed upon readily."[6] By publicity, Hayden said he meant that the state would tell individuals who asked about a stock about the "means of getting data concerning any securities that came out." Too much disclosure and too free the access to company information was a problem, however, for "there must be new enterprises, and we know that the very life of some of those operations is privacy."[7] An insolvent company could also be exempted from disclosure requirements since "Its securities may even then be not wholly worthless, and it is desirable in the public interest to leave some room for the rehabilitation of such a concern."[8] The law should propose penalties for fraud and improper conduct, as long as they did not knowingly and willfully lie about their promises of future dividends, or their assets and liabilities or income.[9] In all, "We would find that ninety per cent of the business of members of this association would be entirely outside the operation of the law and one hundred per cent of the business of really 'Blue Sky Men' would be within the purview of the law," he said.[10]

Hard as it might be to imagine an even more perfunctory oversight—and one that almost certainly was intended to bolster established securities firms' place in the market for financial services rather than to protect the public—it seemed to many of the investment bankers' allies a major concession. "Only a few short years ago such a proposal would have been rejected emphatically as worse than paternalism, as the most radical populism," the *Washington Herald* wrote, adding: "We can see no danger, we anticipate nothing but benefits."[11] Legislators in the state of Maine, aiming to become a center for incorporations in competition with Delaware and New Jersey, quickly enacted a proposal on these lines Hayden suggested. It included no requirement that a securities firm provide a list of securities to be sold or data on assets and earnings. As long as the Bank Commissioner was satisfied that the offerings were made "in good faith ... without intent to deceive or defraud" and that any information the Commissioner chose to require was disclosed to buyers, the offering could proceed.[12] The investment bankers' model, as adopted in Maine, did not include the sweeping authority granted to the Kansas Commissioner to investigate and bar an offering on a finding that a company's articles of incorporation, bylaws, business plan, or contracts were "unfair, unjust, inequitable or oppressive to any class of contributors," or that "does not intend to do a fair and honest business, and in his judgment does not promise a fair return on the stocks, bonds or other securities by it offered for sale."[13]

With limited popular success tagging Blue Sky laws as paternalism or in arguing for their licensing bill, the investment bankers turned to the courts, counting on judicial faith in the *caveat emptor* doctrine. The lead case, challenging Michigan's law, came from Alabama and New Orleans Transportation Co., which operated a railroad link between Tuscaloosa, Alabama, and New Orleans. It had been selling preferred stock and first and second mortgage bonds in Michigan, and the owner of some of its first mortgage bonds wanted to resell them. The railroad was solvent, it had ample assets to support its securities and it argued that having to comply with the Michigan law violated its Constitutional rights—although neither its own offering nor the bond-holder's resale had in fact been rejected. It was the requirement to file and await approval that the railroad found objectionable. Specifically, it said the law deprived it of its property without due process of law as well as its right to equal protection under the act, since the law exempted Michigan banks from its requirements. In addition, the railroad said the law violated the clause in the Constitution that empowers Congress to regulate interstate commerce (eliding the point that states may do so if Congress does not).[14]

The three-judge panel that heard the case said it was taking notice that the Blue Sky law was "intended ... 'to stop the sale of stock in fly-by-night concerns, visionary oil wells, distant gold mines and other like fraudulent exploitations'," but added that even if the law had in fact done so, the railroad was an established company. Moreover, the judges continued, the Blue Sky law did not only address fraud, as it "reaches and prohibits the sale of securities that are honest, valid, and safe" for "it prevents the experienced investor from deliberately assisting an enterprise which he thinks gives sufficient promise of gain to offset the risk of loss."[15] It meant the state was stepping in between willing buyer and willing seller, to substitute its judgment for theirs and so infringe their liberty. The judges also noted that the Blue Sky law could strike a blow to Michigan's economy, by barring a growing automobile firm or furniture maker from raising necessary funds unless the state approved—and if it did not, the firms would have to liquidate. In a direct allusion to the miniature capital markets of self-contained rural communities—that vision that was at the heart of Dolley's paternalism—the judges added:

> If, through local pride or in the effort to save an existing investment or for any indirect benefit to come, the citizens of a town wish to take stock or bonds in a local company, though knowing they are likely to lose their investment and being willing to take the chance, yet they may not; this law forbids.[16]

The issue was whether the Blue Sky law was a legitimate exercise of the police power—whether, that is, it bore a "real or substantial relation to the public welfare." On this point, the judges held, with respect to a company's sale of securities:

> no one can suppose is a public or quasi public enterprise; the business of buying and selling stocks and bonds and other securities is no more 'affected by a public interest' than is the business of buying and selling groceries...[17]

although in fact one of the few exemptions to *caveat emptor* was that buyers of spoiled foodstuffs could be compensated since statutes dating back to Henry VII barred such sales.

Making precisely the same case against West Virginia's Kansas model law, Smith H. Bracey, president of a company selling stock in a small North Carolina gold mine that had stopped production more than seventy years earlier, also followed the investment bankers' script. Here, too, as for the Alabama and New Orleans bonds, he and his Howie Mining Company had not been denied permission to sell shares. Bracey, like the railroad, had not even tried to apply for authorization under the Blue Sky Law.[18] He was saying he was harmed by state action when in fact no action had occurred; he had no idea whether the state would have allowed sale of the stock, though it is likely that his knowledge of what he was really intending would have led him to make a good guess.

The West Virginia judges in Bracey's case accepted all three prongs of the investment bankers' argument against Blue Sky laws: denial of due process to secure property rights, denial of equal protection under law, and violation of the interstate commerce clause of the Constitution, a broader finding than in Michigan.[19] One of the judges on the panel hearing the West Virginia case, however, dissented and held that "in view of the evil which the legislature intended to prevent" the Blue Sky aw was a legitimate effort of the state to protect its citizens.[20] Bracey, continuing his sales, would be sued three years later for defrauding a West Virginia man by selling him $25,000 of stock in the mine with a claim that the played out mine was worth $3 million to $4 million. The promoter was acquitted—caveat emptor was confirmed—and then stiffed his lawyer.[21]

The investment bankers' script also worked when three securities firms challenged Iowa's law, with its narrower focus than the Kansas model that Michigan and West Virginia had adopted. These firms, too, like the Alabama and New Orleans railroad and Bracey, had not actually been denied permission to sell securities. The issue for them was licensing, which they had not formally sought, and which had not been denied. Licensing, the plaintiffs said, deprived them of a property right: their ability to sell shares. Here, the judges held that "to protect the humble, honest citizens of the state, unlearned in the intricacy of business affairs" from "unscrupulous, cunning, and deceitful 'Get-Rich-Quick-Wallingford'" was laudable, the Blue Sky law violated both the commerce clause and the Constitutional guarantee of equal protection under the law.[22] "There are many good men opposed to the 'blue sky' law and paternalistic legislation in general, but it is the truth that every swindler in Iowa was inspired with new hope" with this ruling, one Iowa editor resignedly commented.[23]

At the same time investment bankers won these cases, their apparent willingness to accept a degree of oversight encouraged many state banking officials to hope for a compromise approach that was not as broad as Dolley's. Investment Bankers Association officials met with representatives from National Association of Supervisors of State Banks to negotiate the terms of model legislation in 1914, saying they wanted only not to be included in laws that aimed at "blue sky fakirs, and get-rich-quick concerns." They said regulators should focus on detecting and punishing fraud and argued with Kansas model law or even simply licensing "a successful fraud may pose as an investment bonanza and reap a dishonest harvest under the sanction of the state." In short, the investment bankers' lead lawyer said: "We ask business freedom for the investment dealer, and a rocky road to the county jail for the get-rich-quick promoter."[24]

The model that the investment bankers and the banking superintendents negotiated in fact took an even more permissive step away from Hayden's proposal: rather than registering dealers, the model said any person or company selling securities needed merely to notify a designated state official and to provide copies of any prospectus or circular to be used in the sales effort. That state official could at his or her discretion investigate people selling securities to see if they were defrauding investors. A local prosecutor would then file charges and if convicted, the person or entity could be fined up to $5,000.[25]

Even this proved too rigorous for securities firms as their lobbyists began making their cases before state legislatures. The first state to enact a version of the model, Virginia, dropped the notification and prospectus-filing language.[26] (Virginia would later adopt a Kansas-style merit review; this would, in the 1970s, mean the DeLorean Motor Company's initial share offering, blessed by federal regulators, was barred in Virginia.[27]) Those who spoke for the victims of worthless stock promotions despaired, as states seemed ready to retreat from the Kansas Blue Sky Act model. It seemed as if nothing could protect the public's savings. "No one disputes the necessity of protecting the thrifty and too often gullible investor," a North Dakota paper wrote. "The mails, the growth of advertising and the widely circulated daily press have given the grafter ample opportunity to sell his wares to the unsuspecting. There must be a way out of the difficulty."[28]

Despite the North Dakota editor's gloom and the investment bankers' court victories, the state lawyers who went to court to defend Blue Sky laws continued to have confidence in Dolley's regulatory model. Several state attorneys general declined to go along with the investment bankers' legislation and instead drafted their own proposal for oversight of securities sales. They aimed for more than pursuing cases of fraud. Their model bill said state officials could step in before a securities firm or company directly selling its own shares began offering shares to look at marketing material for the kind of wishful thinking behind batteries that did not work or wireless phones that had not yet been invented. The model law then said that when such not-quite outright lies would "work a fraud" on the buyer, the state had grounds to ban an offering; the fraud, that is, did not have to occur, and the power to ban was not simply to ban false statements but also misleading or improbable ones.[29]

Judges in rural states, too, were unimpressed by investment bankers' charges that Kansas model laws embodied un-American paternalism and imposed an unconstitutional burden on legitimate business. Kansas courts, for instance, had brushed aside challenges to the Blue Sky Act from land contract promoter Don Moun Day and one of his sales agents. "It is no hardship," Atchison County District Court Judge W.A. Jackson concluded,

> "to say to him that before he deals with the people where the chances of practicing fraud and deceit are many, he must satisfy some representative of the people that his dealings are on the square,"

when he rejected an argument by one of Moun Day's sales agents that the Blue Sky act ban denied him his due process rights, levied excessive penalties on him, and gave the Bank Commissioner too much power.[30]

Where then, some judges asked, was the line between fraud and taking advantage—when did the naïve become the sucker? In considering a challenge to National Mercantile Co., a Vancouver, British Columbia firm that was marketing its "Loan and home purchase contracts," an Oregon judge banned the company from selling shares after a "a cursory examination of the scheme under which the company makes its supposed loans and prosecutes its project." The investment scheme National sold (without benefit of registration under Oregon's Blue Sky Act) promised mortgage loans for applicants who made monthly payments into funding pool. The buyers committed to making one hundred monthly payments, to eventually total as much as $5,000, into funding pool. After the first ten payments, an "investor" could draw that sum from the pool, repaying principal at $7 month (on top of the monthly payments already due under the contract) plus interest at a modest sounding three percent. For someone with a $5,000 contract who drew from the pool a $500 mortgage, that meant an annual debt service expense equal to 19.8 percent of the loan over five years before making a final payment of $80 to retire the loan—and all that while continuing to pay $50 a month into the pool, a calculation that few victims likely made.[31]

What made this problematic was not misrepresentation, the Oregon judge suggested, but that its victims clearly did not understand what those terms entailed. Such misunderstanding was not enough under the caveat emptor rule to reverse a transaction, but it was becoming grounds enough for a paternalistically inclined state and courts to opt for a new way to deal with sales that were carefully designed to deceive without necessarily meeting a legal definition of fraud. In Montana, U.S. District Court Judge George Bourquin upheld a ban on National Mercantile on the grounds that it violated the state's Blue Sky law requirement that securities offer fair deals to buyers. There was no Constitutional issue, whether of property rights, equal protection under law, or interstate commerce, Bourquin ruled in banning the company from operating, for "All this is settled law since the classic case wherein one highwayman of two operating upon Blackheath near London came into chancery for an accounting of profits accruing from their villainy.".[32]

In any event, popular support for Blue Sky law protection was not discouraged by the court decisions in Iowa, Michigan, and West Virginia overturning those states' laws. "If the many thousands of men and who have lost in plunges in mining stocks, in oil and other promotions vote as they feel," an effort to overturn California's Blue Sky law would fail, one editor commented—and in fact, it would.[33] After North Carolina's Supreme Court upheld that state's Blue Sky law barring "foreign vendors of worthless 'securities' …The zeal with which State Insurance Commissioner [James R.] Young keeps after that tribe of frauds … has well nigh cleaned 'em out," one editor commented, adding that hundreds North Carolinians had "dropped piles of good money for a lot of junk and rubbish" every year.[34]

What the people who Kansas model Blue Sky laws sought to protect really wanted when buying stock was a way to earn a return on their savings. Their focus was on security and safety and they were unconcerned with the idea that they were making possible the future growth of that enterprise. They wanted, that is, the analogue to the regular interest payment that clipping coupons on a bond offered or that the rate promised by the local bank or building and loan society. That was not what the Bargain Store's stockholders wanted; for them, shares of stock represented ownership stakes were meant to give them a voice in running the business as well as a share of any profit. Nor was this what Americans sought in the post-World War I stock market boom, when a churn of buying and selling seemed to offer unending profit—until October 1929 and the great Wall Street crash. It was the concept of share ownership as a more high-powered version of an interest-bearing savings account that, for the public and legislators, justified Blue Sky law paternalism.

The get-rich-quick promoters' promises of double-digit (or even triple-digit) percentage dividends made a different kind of appeal than the one that attracted individuals with easy access to brokerage officers in major financial centers looked at owning shares: there, the pitch was the opportunity to make money buying shares (often on margin, with just a small sum as a down payment) and quickly selling them for a profit. Tales like one about Thomas Edison's backer, Nathan G. Miller, who went from the family farm in Connecticut with a $700 inheritance to New York, where he "developed a talent for high finance" and made a fortune on the stock market, or Louis Lombard, who saved his nickels as a street musician, opened a music school, accumulated $60,000 from it, "put the money in Wall Street and made a clean-up of millions," started many people thinking in new ways about shares—even as they criticized "Bet-A-Million" Gates" multi-million-dollar profits speculating in railroad shares.[35]

Yet, even as Blue Sky laws and their enforcers continued to focus on deals that appealed to the traditional view that shares of stock were to be held and that the dividends they paid were what mattered, speculation on changes in the price of shares quoted on a stock exchange was becoming a possibility as enticing, if not more so, than a dividend. The stock and bond promotions that were the focus of Kansas model Blue Sky laws did not trade so easily, if indeed they could be traded at all. When the promoters of this type of stock promised, as so many did, a rise in price they meant (and said) the rise would come simply by an act of a company's board of directors. The people Blue Sky laws sought to protect did not necessarily understand that those price declarations meant nothing if they could not really sell their shares. The target of Kansas model Blue Sky law was speculation in hopes of unrealistic prospects of dividend yield. The laws missed the growing (if unrealistic) attraction of riches from speculation when trading shares.

When, finally, Blue Sky laws came before the U.S. Supreme Court, its ruling that they were legitimate exercises of police power in rulings came too late to really matter much. Chicago-based investment bank N.W. Halsey & Co., Weis Fiber Container Corporation, a manufacturer that sold its own shares directly and large group of securities firms challenged Michigan's revised Blue Sky law, claiming "There has nowhere at any time been any suggestion of any wide-spread fraud" in stock and bond sales and that Michigan's law unfairly burdened business.[36] The high court, ever sensitive to popular sentiment, was unconvinced. Justice

Joseph McKenna, writing for an eight to one majority, held that the Michigan law "burdens honest business, it is true, but burdens it only that under its forms dishonest business may not be done." To reject a law because it caused expense and inconvenience would make states impotent to carry out their functions, for "It costs something to be governed."[37] Upholding the state's ability to step in to protect savings, McKenna made the point that honest dealing was something more than simply not telling a lie.

In a parallel case, decided the same day, challenging Ohio's Blue Sky law, like Michigan's a variation of the Kansas model meant to address earlier federal court objections, McKenna rejected arguments by a securities firm and an automobile company that the law puts investors "under guardianship"—that it was too paternalistic—because it "shields contemplating purchasers from loss of property by the exercise of their own defective judgment."[38] States had the power to exercise "unsolicited protection," McKenna wrote, "and there is much in the business we are considering" to suggest such paternalism is appropriate. "It is not wise to put out of view the tendencies" of a business that "tempts to and facilitates speculative judgments." While the law could not bar speculation, "against counterfeits of value the law can give protection" and Blue Sky law "must be judged of upon that consideration, not upon the assertion of an absolute liberty of conduct which does not exist."[39] Paternalism was fine, when Mr. Thompkins came to town. But more and more often, the public was entranced by other tales.

Notes

1. Kenneth Wiggins Porter, "The Business Man in American Folklore," *Bulletin of the Business Historical Society*, Vol. 18, No. 5 (November 1944): 126.
2. Johnson Brigham, *The Banker in Literature* (New York: Bankers Publishing Co, 1910): 243–244.
3. Booth Tarkington, *The Magnificent Ambersons* (Garden City, NY: Doubleday, Page, 1918): 79–80.
4. "Political Gossip," *Topeka State Journal*, February 28, 1914: 6; "Snapshots," Ibid., October 20, 1920: 6; "Dolly Files Papers," *Topeka Daily Capital*, June 17, 1924: 7; Dolley's view on western "financiering" is from "To Go It Alone," *Topeka State Journal*, October 13, 1910: 5; for the argument that Dolly was basically

looking out for bankers see, e.g., "Blue Sky Law Not Popular," *Salt Lake Tribune* (Salt Lake City, Utah) March 26, 1913: 10; Macey and Miller, "Origin of the Blue Sky Laws," and Paul G. Mahoney, "The Origins of the Blue-Sky Laws: A Test of Competing Hypotheses," *The Journal of Law & Economics*, Vol. 46, No. 1 (April 2003): 229–251.

5. Proceedings, annual convention of the Investment bankers' association of America, 1912, 140–141.
6. Ibid., 145.
7. Ibid., 146.
8. Ibid.
9. Ibid., 147.
10. Ibid.
11. "Bankers and the Blue Sky Law," *Washington Herald* November 29, 1912: 6. The Herald thought the most essential part of the IBA model law was a requirement that companies making offerings of stocks or bonds file financial statements with state officials, which in theory could be inspected by individuals interested in buying shares—that is, that the statements would not have to be provided directly to potential purchasers. In the event, the neither the District of Columbia nor its Congressional overlords ever enacted any regulation, and Washington was a hot spot for securities fraud well into the 1930s.
12. Maine Revised Statutes 1913, chapter 209, sections 1, 2, 8, 9.
13. An Act to provide for the regulation and supervision of investment companies and providing penalties for the violation thereof, Kansas Session Laws 1911, chapter 133, sec. 5.
14. Alabama & New Orleans Transportation Co. v. Doyle, 210 Fed. 173 (U.S. District Court, Eastern District of Michigan, 1914), at 177–178.
15. Ibid., at 175.
16. Ibid.
17. Ibid., 180.
18. "Blue Sky Law is Defended by Darst," *The Daily Telegram* (Clarksburg. West Virginia) August 25, 1914: 10; Bracey et al. v Darst, state Auditor of West Virginia 218 F. 482 (U.S. District Court, northern district of West Virginia, 1914) at 496.
19. Bracey v Darst at 482, 495–496; "Certainly it is within the power as it is clearly the duty of the State to limit and regulate the powers

and operations of Corporations," the Florida court ruled, adding that the dealer's contention that he was denied equal protection of the laws also did not have merit because the Blue Sky involved "the public welfare and is applicable alike to all corporations." Ex Parte C.H. Taylor 68 Fla. 61 (Florida Supreme Court, 1914) at 61, 73.

20. Bracey v Darst, at 497.
21. "Bracey is Held to Grand Jury," *Wheeling (West Virginia) Intelligencer*, February 13, 1917: 5; Frank A. O'Brian vs Smith H. Bracey, Ibid., May 19, 1920: 10.
22. William R. Compton Co. v. Allen, 216 F. 537 (U.S. District Court, Southern District of Iowa 1914), at 538, 545, 547 (per curiam), cert. dismissed, 239 U.S. 652 (1915).
23. "Iowa Press Comment," *The Denison (Iowa) Review*, February 25, 1914: 2.
24. Robert Reed, "Report of General Counsel," Proceedings, Annual convention of the Investment Bankers' Association of America (Chicago, 1915), 187.
25. Ibid., 191–193.
26. An Act to prevent unfairness, imposition or fraud in the issuance, sale, promotion, negotiation, or distribution of any stocks, bonds, notes, or other securities or contracts, Virginia Acts of Assembly, 1916. Chap 499.
27. David Ress, "On the SCC's Front Line for Consumer Protection," *Richmond (Virginia) Times-Dispatch*, October 1, 2022: 1.
28. "Blue Sky Laws," *Bismarck (North Dakota) Daily Tribune*, December 1, 1915: 4.
29. Act No. 46, Laws of 1915, section 2 (c). For discussion of the 1915 law's modifications from the original 1913 Kansas model bill, see Robert R. Reed and Lester H. Washburn, *Blue Sky Laws: Analysis and Text* (New York: Clark Boardman Co., 1921):64 The idea that caveat emptor might not apply to securities was previously confirmed in Meyer v. Richards, 163 U.S. 385 (U.S. Supreme Court, 1896).
30. "Blue Sky Law OK," *The Hays (Kansas) Free Press*, March 14, 1914: 3.
31. National Mercantile Co.Ltd v Watson, Corporation Commissioner, 215 F. 929 (U.S. District Court, Oregon, 1914) at 930.
32. National Mercantile Co. Ltd. v Keating, State Auditor of Montana, 218 F. 477 (U.S. District Court, Montana, 1914) at 479.

33. "The Blue Sky Law," *The Call* (San Francisco), June 6, 1913: 6.
34. "Chances of Various Candidates as Viewed by a Raleigh Scribe," *The Commonwealth* (Scotland Neck, North Carolina) May 16, 1916: 1.
35. "Good Advice Not Wasted," *Fergus County Democrat* (Lewiston, Montana) September 6, 1910: 6, "Dad Said Git," *Holbrook (Arizona) News*, November 4, 1910: 2; "Man Who Fiddled His Way To Fortune," *The Hattiesburg (Mississippi) News*, December 13, 1916: 3.
36. Merrick v. N. W. Halsey & Co., 242 U.S. 568 (U.S.Supreme Court, 1917) at 580.
37. Ibid., at 587.
38. Hall v. Geiger-Jones Co., 242 U.S. 539 (U.S. Supreme Court, 1917 at 554, referring to Ohio Revised Code (1917) § 6373–6376.
39. Ibid., at 554–555.

Bibliography

Alabama & New Orleans Transportation Co. v. Doyle, 210 Fed. 173 (U.S. District Court, Eastern District of Michigan, 1914).

An Act to provide for the regulation and supervision of investment companies and providing penalties for the violation thereof, Kansas Session Laws 1911, chapter 133.

Act No. 46, Unfairness, Imposition or Fraud in the Sale of Securities: So-called "Blue Sky" Law, Kansas Session Laws of 1915, chapter 164.

Maine Revised Statutes 1913, chapter 209.

An Act to prevent unfairness, imposition or fraud in the issuance, sale, promotion, negotiation, or distribution of any stocks, bonds, notes or other securities or contracts, Virginia Acts of Assembly, 1916. Chap 499.

Anonymous. 1910a. "Good Advice Not Wasted," *Fergus County Democrat* (Lewiston, Montana) September 6: 6

———. 1910b. "To Go It Alone," *Topeka State Journal*, October 13: 5.

———. 1910c. "Dad Said Git," *Holbrook (Arizona) News*, November 4: 2.

———. 1912. "Bankers and the Blue Sky Law," *Washington Herald*, November 29: 6.

———. 1913a. "Blue Sky Law Not Popular," *Salt Lake Tribune* (Salt Lake City, Utah) March 26: 10.

———. 1913b. "The Blue Sky Law," *The Call* (San Francisco), June 6: 6.

———. 1914a. "Iowa Press Comment," *The Denison (Iowa) Review*, February 25: 2.

———. 1914b. "Political Gossip," *Topeka State Journal*, February 28: 6.

———. 1914c. "Blue Sky Law OK," *The Hays (Kansas) Free Press*, March 14: 3.

———. 1914d. "Blue Sky Law is Defended by Darst," *The Daily Telegram* (Clarksburg. West Virginia) August 25: 10.

———. 1915. "Blue Sky Laws," *Bismarck (North Dakota) Daily Tribune*, December 1: 4.

———. 1916a. "Chances of Various Candidates as Viewed by a Raleigh Scribe," *The Commonwealth,* (Scotland Neck, North Carolina) May 16: 1.

———. 1916b. "Man Who Fiddled His Way To Fortune," *The Hattiesburg (Mississippi) News*, December 13: 3.

———. 1917. "Bracey is Held to Grand Jury," *Wheeling (West Virginia) Intelligencer*, February 13: 5.

———. 1920a. "Frank A. O'Brian vs Smith H. Bracey," *Wheeling (West Virginia) Intelligencer*, May 19: 10.

———. 1920b. "Snapshots," *Topeka State Journal*, October 20: 6.

———. 1924. "Dolly Files Papers," *Topeka Daily Capital*, June 17: 7.

Bracey et al. v Darst, state Auditor of West Virginia 218 F. 482 (U.S. District Court, northern district of West Virginia, 1914).

Brigham, Johnson. 1910. *The Banker in Literature*. New York: Bankers Publishing Co, 1910.

William R. Compton Co. v. Allen, 216 F. 537 (U.S. District Court, Southern District of Iowa 1914).

Hall v. Geiger-Jones Co., 242 U.S. 539 (U.S. Supreme Court, 1917).

Investment Bankers Association. 1912. *Proceedings of the Organization Meeting and of the First Annual Convention of the Investment Bankers' Association of America* Chicago: Investment Bankers Association.

Jonathan R. Macey Jonathan R. & Geoffrey P. Miller. 1991. "Origin of the Blue Sky Laws," *Texas Law Review*, 70: 348–397.

Mahoney, Paul G. 2003. "The Origins of the Blue-Sky Laws: A Test of Competing Hypotheses," *The Journal of Law & Economics*, 46: 229–251.

Merrick v. N. W. Halsey & Co., 242 U.S. 568 (U.S. Supreme Court, 1917).

National Mercantile Co. Ltd. v Keating, State Auditor of Montana, 218 F. 477 (U.S. District Court, Montana, 1914).

National Mercantile Co. Ltd v Watson, Corporation Commissioner, 215 F. 929 (U.S. District Court, Oregon, 1914).

Porter, Kenneth Wiggins. 1944. "The Business Man in American Folklore," *Bulletin of the Business Historical Society*, 18: 126.

Reed, Robert. 1915. "Report of General Counsel," Proceedings, Annual convention of the Investment Bankers' Association of America Chicago: Investment Bankers Association, 187–193.

Reed Robert & Lester H. Washburn. 1921. *Blue Sky Laws: Analysis and Text*. New York: Clark Boardman Co.

Ex Parte C.H. Taylor 68 Fla. 61 (Florida Supreme Court, 1914).

CHAPTER 8

Securities Speculation on the Rise: Still Falling for Dreams of Wealth

Abstract As Americans' interest in stock market trading grew in the 1920s, the arguments of investment bankers that Kansas model regulation was paternalistic tapped into a growing sense that government regulation was an infringement of liberty. Economists' insistence that markets could regulate themselves also undermined faith in securities regulation, even as ever-larger frauds were sold to a public that was losing millions on offerings.

Keywords Speculation · Investment banking · Wall Street · Stock exchanges

In arguing for his Blue Sky law, Dolley had declared that fraud; "fakirs" and fake stocks were his target. He in fact sought and won the power to prohibit offerings that seemed to him to be unfair, unduly speculative or that were more like than not to lose buyers much or all of their savings. The conflation of fraud—of lying—with marketing that counted on the target's lack of knowledge or experience made legislators, and at least some judges, comfortable with a relatively heavy-handed state intervention in individuals' management of their financial affairs. Moreover, at least some Blue Sky law administrators saw their role as not merely that of preventing loss. Minnesota's commission, for instance, declared in its

D. Ress, *The Kansas Blue Sky Act of 1911*,
https://doi.org/10.1007/978-3-031-43831-8_8

1918 annual report that it "has interpreted the law to mean that the sale of a security is fraudulent, or tends to work a fraud on the purchaser, if the latter does not have a fair chance to gain by his investment. It is not sufficient that the money invested is secure against loss."

This approach, the lead lawyer for the Investment Bankers Association's campaign against Blue Sky laws argued, would apply not only "to the promotion of a mining property in Mexico, a railroad in China" but also to a business hoping to sell a new kind of automobile, or hoping to gain from a franchise or contract that involved legal risks "or any other enterprise, the future of which is wholly speculative, a matter of individual judgment or guesswork." In fact, he said, in one court case challenging a Blue Sky law, "It was admitted in oral argument … that the promotion of the Ford automobile, which was originally financed as a pure speculation and considered visionary by business men, would probably have been disapproved under these laws" (Ford Motor Co. was originally financed through a partnership agreement between Henry Ford and a wealthy coal dealer, who later brought in ten business associates, including a firm that sold parts to Ford, through a $74,500 private placement. This type of financing, very much in the style, if much larger in scale, of the launch of the Bargain Store in Dodge City or Dolley's ventures into the Stockgrowers State Bank or the Maple Hill blacksmith he backed in his earliest days in Kansas, would have been exempt under most Blue Sky laws in effect at the time).

At the Kansas Bank Commissioner's office, the pace of applications also picked up. During the twelve months ended June 30, 1919, a total of 158 firms applied to the Kansas Bank Commissioner for permission to sell nearly $98.5 million worth of securities; of these, the Commissioner refused to approve 52 while three firms withdrew their applications. The remaining 103 were given permission to sell, but with sales limited to $24 million worth of shares—the difference being "water which the board forced promoters to wring out," commissioner Walter E. Wilson told the Topeka Rotary Club. He said he and his staff probably saved Kansans an additional $100 million, on top of the $74 million in disapproved and scaled back offerings, because other promoters became discouraged after consulting with the banking department and never bothered to apply for an offering. "Had it not been for the restrictions of this law it is safe to assume that the striking of oil in the mid-continent field would literally have swamped this commonwealth with stock selling pirates who would have robbed our people of millions of dollars," he said.[1]

There was an important difference between what the Bank Commissioner was seeing and what Kansans saw when reading New York Stock Exchange prices in a daily paper. The Banking Commissioner approved stock offerings of two hundred twenty firms during the decade after 1917 when Kansas began requiring the founders of a firm seeking to sell shares to the public put their stock in escrow, as a way of insuring offerings were not simply a device for promoters to profit at investors' expense. More than half of the firms depositing shares with the Kansas Bank Commissioner had their permits pulled without the shares being returned because the firms had gone under, sometimes in just a few months, as when the Banking Commission canceled the permit granted Automobile Lock and Alarm Company of Topeka five months after its two principals put their $8,200 of shares into escrow.[2]

The number of offerings approved in Kansas was roughly the same number of shares as were traded on the New York Stock Exchange, although mix of firms on each list were markedly different. All but nine of approved companies in Kansas were Kansan companies; almost all were oil and gas ventures, which sought additional funds from the public's money after organizers' initial investments of as little as the $1,200 that eight friends and neighbors put into Northern Pottawatomie Oil and Gas Company in 1918; this firm's permit was pulled seven years later. The blue chip and established firms on the New York exchange did not bother to seek the Kansas Bank Commissioner's approval. They had no need to. Investors from across the nation (including Kansas) easily phoned in orders to trade more than 20,000 shares a day in such firms as U.S. Steel, General Motors, Studebaker, Willys-Overland and U.S. Rubber, none of which filed with the state banking commission.

There was, even in the state with the toughest Blue Sky Act, plenty of opportunity for people to bet on the most speculative of ventures. The Blue Sky Act, moreover, did not discourage investment in Kansan companies or slow the state's growth, despite the challenge that Kansas was dependent on a staple shipped almost entirely out of state—wheat—with only limited backward in-state linkages to input industries such as farm equipment or fertilizer or to forward linkages to processors to generate economic growth.[3] Manufacturers' capital in Kansas grew by 129 percent between 1909 and 1919, compared to 116 percent in New York and 130 percent in Massachusetts, both financial centers that had emphatically rejected Blue Sky law regulation as an unnecessary constraint on capital formation. Production output grew by 181 percent in Kansas compared to 163 percent in New York and 169 percent in Massachusetts. Michigan, with its Kansas model Blue Sky Act, saw a 301 percent increase business capital and a 406 percent increase in the value of its output.[4]

The Kansas legislature, meanwhile, had shored up Dolley's law with a series of amendments in 1915 law amendments detailing seven specific grounds for rejecting an offering, including deceptive advertising, share prices in excess of the per share value of the offeror's assets and that a business was "a mere scheme of a promoter or promoters to get rich quick at the expense of the purchasers."[5] Kansas courts had brushed aside challenges that the original act gave too much power to a single executive branch official, the Bank Commissioner, and they continued to reject notions about caveat emptor as they upheld the Blue Sky law.[6] The Kansas Supreme Court upheld the conviction of stock promoter R. J. Bell for making false statements about an oil company's finances, confirmed the decision to invalidate an issue of shares to an oil company officer, invalidated a note when the maker did not obtain a Blue Sky law permit, and held that the buyer of securities in a firm that proved worthless could get his money back from the company's officers because the firm did not have a state permit to sell shares in Kansas.[7]

Kansas was particularly strict. In the first two years after Michigan's legislature enacted its Blue Sky law, the review panel comprising the Attorney General, State Treasurer, and Bank Commissioner received 527 applications to sell securities, approved 451 and refused 23.[8] The rest were either still pending review or withdrawn before the panel acted—that is, the panel found five percent of proposed offerings were inappropriate options for the public's savings. The following year it received another 245 applications and approved 181. These, like the Kansas approvals, tended to be different sorts of enterprises than were listed in New York, with an average value for each offering of about $330,000. Of the more than $27 million worth of shares the Michigan board allowed, on condition that proceeds were to be held in escrow until the stock paid (fairly hefty) annual dividends of six percent, most never reached this level. Some $24 million was returned to investors.[9] Michigan, too, was willing to allow speculation, but speculation with insurance against loss. Risk was not going to fall only on the party in these transactions with the more limited knowledge; *caveat emptor* would not apply. The standard for performance was high, too: in contrast to Michigan's six percent dividend requirement, American Tobacco, a monopoly, paid a five percent dividend. Capital formation after enactment of the Michigan law increased by

301 percent between 1909 and 1919, and industrial production rose 406 percent, with both far outpacing growth in non-Blue Sky law states.[10]

In the first two years of the Nebraska securities bureau's operations, it approved $89.8 million of stock offerings and denied 136 requests to sell a total of $42.5 million face value of shares—tiny issues, that is, on a scale that was orders of magnitude smaller than even the smallest stock exchange listed securities that could be bought with a simple telegraphed or telephoned order. The Nebraska bureau denied another $15.2 million worth of stock before the promoters even applied for a permit. While most companies approved ended up being viable investments, some $1.3 million (face value) of approved offerings were for shares in companies that quickly ended up in bankruptcy or were in obviously doubtful financial condition. Failed and faltering companies rejected offerings and the offerings that were banned even without filing for state authorization amounted to about forty percent of the deals proposed to Nebraska residents.[11] Nebraska capital formation and value of production also outpaced New York and Massachusetts, with a 146 percent increase in business capital and a 199 percent increase in output.[12]

Some offerings, however, reached Nebraskans without benefit of a state permit. The Missouri Valley Cattle Loan Company's promoters targeted wealthy farmers, business owners, and bankers with face-to-face sales calls, supplementing their statewide newspaper advertisements (in German and Czech, as well as English), which falsely claimed "We Are Already Doing Business ... Our Books Are Recording Profits Every Day."[13] It was a scam much like one the promoters had already worked, selling shares in a potash mill that never opened. Even when individuals who were somewhat more wary about stock promotions, like C. C. Carek, cashier of the Bank of Touhy, questioned the legality of the potash company offerings, they could be fairly easily reassured. Those big dividends were hard to resist. In Carek's case, one of the offering's primary promoters, William H. McWhorter, drove the sixty miles from Omaha to the banker's hamlet to say he had applied for a stock sales permit. Carek did not seem to realize (or perhaps to care) that McWhorter needed to have that permit in hand before trying to sell any shares.[14] The promoters' main approach to their victims was through bankers and cattle ranchers who "acted as 'bird dogs' or 'pointers' and it was in these conversations that company's promises of thirty-two percent annual dividends were floated. The people who fell for this were relatively wealthy rural business owners and farmers such as W. B. Johnson and a Mr. Alexander, who gave cash and notes amounting to $7,251 and $10,000, respectively, for shares.[15]

West Virginia's revised Blue Sky law cleared the way for prosecutors to charge a Morgantown stock dealer who took a commission of more than ten percent on sales of Gilchrist Drug Co. stock. And while securities officials found F. W. Sysley was selling the shares for $3 when they were trading in the company's Pittsburgh home base for $1.65, promising Morgantown residents that if he raised $30,000 at his "cut price" offer, the company would open a drug store in the town, Sysley left town before he could be served with a summons to appear in court. Prosecutors in Martinsburg, West Virginia, pursued M. L. Mishine who had been selling shares in a company he said had raised $7 million to build an automobile plant in Cumberland, Maryland. A Mrs. Frank Snyder complained that she and her husband bought shares after being promised the stock would jump in price by 25 percent over the next fifteen days. The factory was never completed, and the company produced a grand total of four prototypes.[16] There were still plenty of speculative ventures available in Blue Sky law states for those willing to assume the risk. West Virginia's capital formation, up 124 percent between 1909 and 1919 and output, up 191 percent, seem to have been unconstrained by its Blue Sky Act.[17]

There were even more such ventures in supposedly more sophisticated states, where legislators felt Dolley's approach was too paternalistic. Despite faith in tales of the American sharp-witted dealer, when states rejected the Kansan model of merit review on the grounds that their citizens, when information was available could look out for themselves, it seemed that in many cases they could not. Promoters seized on this: An Ohio firm launched as the sales arm of the United States Leather Corp (not the same company as the Dow Jones Industrial Average's United States Leather Co.). "appears to be making most of its attempts to sell in New York and Pennsylvania, where there are no Blue Sky Law, and not to be selling in Ohio, where there is Blue Sky Laws," the magazine *United States Investor* somewhat ungrammatically reported. Since United States Leather was not yet producing enough to make a profit, and since the sales firm, set up by a stock promoter named T. G. Selleck, planned to pay cash for goods and sell them on credit "this is a highly hazardous business, and anyone buying the stock of the company, would be taking the risks of an unproven enterprise," the *Investor* noted.[18]

By the time Maryland's Attorney General stepped in to freeze sales of shares in the various L. R. Steel chain store and real estate companies, in order to investigate how the companies' salesmen marketed the stocks, the sales effort had collected $36 million from hopeful investors for enterprises that had assets amounting to about $3 million. "I have been approached by salesmen ... who claim that this company is opening a chain of 5 cent to $1 stores throughout the country, Canada and England," with a promise of a seven percent annual dividend, "M.G.D." wrote to the investment advice columnist of the *New York Tribune* in October, 1920. "In our opinion the stock of the L. R. Steel is too speculative for investment purposes," the columnists replied. "We do not know whether there whether there is so much money going to be made in retailing ... We doubt if there would be a satisfactory market for the stock if you bought it."[19]

Glowing reports from Steel's in-house "Americanadian Service" publication in hand, Steel's army of sales agents had been able to sell new shares of stock at $100 each, doing so even as disappointed holders were trying to unload common shares for as little as $10 and preferred stock for $30: information, including price quotations, were not as widely available as the investment bankers' insistence that disclosure was the best protection for investors. Steel's boasts of his retailing genius and claims of success that other chains did not show, prompted the *United States Investor* to comment that he "left the Metropolitan Stores chain enterprise in a huff" while the company's financial statements "are strangely silent on the subject of actual profits earned." The magazine noted, as the people who bought Steel's shares did not, that thirty cents of dollar of assets reported were intangible leases, goodwill, and organization expenses—the first not reflecting a general slump in rents that year and the last not an asset at all but actually a loss that should have been noted on an income statement. The magazine's earlier reports had noted that some twenty-one cents of every dollar received from the company's recent preferred stock issue went to cover the costs of selling the shares and suggested that it was this offering, in a Ponzi-scheme-like manner, that had funded the dividends Steel had paid. Still, if people were still falling for promises such as the extrapolation of one random, but record sales week revenue to make a glowing projection for the year, the good news, the magazine noted, was that "Meantime, blue sky laws seem to be proving a troublesome obstacle in several states," the magazine noted.

Michigan, it added, banned the sale of Steel's Weeghman venture—a bankrupt "one-arm lunch" cafeteria chain that he had acquired as a vehicle for a separate $10 million offering.[20]

The Michigan commission had also just barred a $1.3 million secondary offering by Eureka Croesus Mining Co., with shares actively traded on the New York Curb Market (predecessor to the American Stock Exchange) and Detroit Stock Exchange, after company President F. L. Torres had told the latest stockholders meeting that "we have available hundreds of thousands of tons of ore which we can deliver ... without employing one miner and using one stick of powder," *United States Investor* reported a few weeks earlier. Michigan's assistant state geologist went to check and told the securities commission that Torres' statement was deliberate attempt to deceive.[21]

Steel pushed his shares in states like Washington and Maryland that did not have Blue Sky laws with the strict kind of merit review the Kansas law did, as well as in states that had no laws at all. The Maryland Attorney General's move came on the basis that Steel's share sales were fraudulent, and his after-the-fact effort to clean up the mess came barely a month before a lawsuit from National Toy and Tinsel Manufacturing Co., seeking payment for products shipped, pushed the companies into bankruptcy in March, 1923.[22] California's law, limited to initial offerings, was unable to prevent the sale of some 4.2 million additional unauthorized shares in Julian Petroleum Co., a textbook example of stock watering. Those shares allowed executives and their financial backers to extract millions from the company before its collapse into receivership, at losses to the buyers of those shares estimated at $100 million.[23]

Jurisdictions that did not have a Blue Sky Act, such as the District of Columbia, left an open field for inappropriate and even deceptive offerings. It was only when curious holders of the Anderson Tire and Rubber Company shares touted by Washington. D.C. promoter Harry B. Thomas decided to come and check the company's plant that he said he had just purchased that "To their surprise they were informed that the plant had not been sold." Here, as with Mr. Thompkins and the Kansas widow, sales were primarily made face to face—some 100 sales agents just in Washington, D.C. Sales agents earned commissions of up to 30 percent. Oklahoma Senator Robert L. Owen sunk $120,000 in the promotion, endorsing notes from banks in Washington, St. Louis, Kansas City, and Oklahoma. As the promoters became aware Post Office inspectors were slowly closing in, they proposed swapping Anderson shares for stock in

Rowe-Stuart Motors, a Pennsylvanian firm that they said Owen partly owned.[24] Other promotions in the District of Columbia included the Crystal Glass Casket Company, which never actually made its promised transparent coffins, and one that raised $3 million selling shares in a company that said it made a "no-axle" automobile. These and similar deals led a District of Columbia grand jury to declare that the District of Columbia was a Mecca for wildcat stock promoters because it had no Blue Sky law.[25]

Still, despite the successes of Blue Sky Act regulation in frustrating many worthless securities swindles, "We are all familiar with the kind of parent whose continued 'don'ts' have only succeeded in stimulating in the child an appetite for the thing so often denied," *U.S. Investor*'s editors reflected. "There may be a suspicion that the blue sky law, by forbidding the sale of this or that security, may have an effect not unlike that of the chiding parent."[26] It would not be long before the magazine's editors would harden their view about Blue Sky laws. They launched 1922 by wondering: "How are we going to draw the fangs of the promoters?" since "In spite of Blue Sky Laws, they continue to ply their trade with great success among thrifty people, more especially those of small means." It was in fact the case that "the worst swindles are no longer being perpetrated," the editors admitted, but added that "The Blue Sky operator has discovered that he must have a more complex story to tell now," helped—though the magazine did not say this—by promoters' focus on trading shares on the nation's fast-growing stock exchanges, especially those, like the Curb Market, with relatively lax listing standards but that nevertheless provided what was becoming the one bit of financial information investors and would-be investors were coming to rely upon: the price of a stock and whether it rose or fell from the day before. This helped made possible, and plausible, schemes like the Eureka Croesus deal that the Michigan commission squashed: that offering was intended as a vehicle for two principals in the company, who had organized a pool of 700,000 shares, to profit through a market manipulation—what would later be called a "pump and dump" maneuver. Telling these sorts of new tales was what mattered, even if United States Investor did not make the connection to the lure of quick profits by trading shares, and "Those who cannot do this, really are driven away by Blue Sky laws," the editors admitted.[27]

Instead, the editors believed a perverse effect of Kansas model state regulation was that Blue Sky laws sheltered clever scamsters by granting them the sanction of the state while at the same time chilling business innovation by barring investment in legitimate if risky ventures. "It takes more than a blue sky law to protect investors," the magazine concluded in a look at Ohio's strict law, while "In Michigan, a scheme for bridging the river that separates Detroit from Canada has been let loose by the state securities commission," the editors reported."There is not merely a possibility but a real probability that thousands will put their savings into this scheme, who have no real perception of the risk they are taking," even though the offering is legal because it "is not an improper speculation for those who can afford to take considerable chances with their money."[28]

In the event, this did not happen. While the first attempt to finance the bridge bankrupted its main promoter, stockbroker Russell T. Scott, one of Scott's partners, John W. Austin of the Detroit Graphite Co. (who saw the bridge as offering a lucrative painting contract for his firm) put together a syndicate that financed what would become the profitable Ambassador Bridge. This syndicate—a big city version of much more modest group that had financed Dodge City's Bargain Store, paid Scott's investors back, including a five percent interest (It is not clear how many of these were the small savers *United States Investor* worried about, since the syndicate that took over, however, was mainly drawn from Detroit and New York financial and cross-border trade interests). Scott's bankruptcy, meanwhile, sent him on a spiral of drug use, eventually to murder a druggist during a robbery; he committed suicide after his conviction for murder and sentence to be hanged.[29]

As it turned out, the federal securities law proposed by Representative Edward Denison, a Republican from southern Illinois, might have allowed public financing of the Detroit bridge if it had passed, since—among many other types of securities—it allowed those secured by mortgages or leases or real estate: a bridge and its approaches had to have permanent places to stand on land, after all. It also allowed railroads, electric, gas and water utilities, banks and trust companies, firms listed on a stock exchange, and firms that had been in operation for at least five years to freely sell securities; others, however, would be banned. Investment banks and life insurance companies, both seeing the law as a way of bolstering their position in the competition for middle class savings, rallied in support, but mining promoters, fueled by a "spirit of protest against paternalism," fought back. They were joined by real estate interests, particularly mortgage brokers, with the Iowa Farm Mortgage Association contending that the act would in effect result in a federal government "endorsement of many kinds of securities of doubtful value" and would promote check fraud. The Iowans said most of the worthless investments that advocates like Davis said were sold through mail solicitation were actually sold by high pressure sales agents dealing face-to-face with their victims, rather as Mr. Thompkins had.[30]

The tale of quashed enterprise that the western miners retailed was quickly taken up by legislators from states where easygoing attitudes to finance and the behavior of corporation directors and executives was good business. "You would have had very little of the development of the mineral resources of the country" if the Denison bill passed, said Representative Caleb R. Layton, Republican of Delaware, a state that had a lucrative sideline with its easy incorporation process that allowed companies the broadest powers and courts that were skeptical about stockholder lawsuits alleging failures of fiduciary duties. "A purely prospective, honestly legitimate undertaking, a belief and faith in mineral resources in the ground, but which have not been proven, can not get upon any of these stock exchanges. That being the case, they cannot get any money there," Layton added.[31]

Denison's bill died. The story that it represented the paternalism of an elite—bureaucrats or Wall Street finance houses, depending—inimical to exactly those American virtues expressed by the bold western venturer was too much for its advocates at a time when accusations of paternalism were finally having more effect. For, as a Federal Council of the Churches of Christ in America text book for Sunday schools and adult Bible study session warned: "The continuation of paternalism can have no other result than the creation of a servile people."[32] Even worse fates could be at stake: "It would be a tragedy," declared Otto Kahn, primary partner of the giant Kuhn Loeb investment bank, if Americans' "ordered and enlightened freedom and covenanted individual rights ...should be invaded by that most insidious foe of liberty, paternalism, with its allies and close relatives, bureaucracy and socialism."[33]

The failure of the Denison bill cleared a path for the further undermining of the state Blue Sky laws, particularly those, as in Kansas, Michigan, and Ohio that were effective protectors of the public. The "spirit of paternalism" in Blue Sky laws reflected a philosophy of "too many idle parlor theorists" who were "smothering the individualism by which this country has grown great," one Ohio securities lawyer complained.[34] After all, the "fundamental act of exchange" between buyer and seller "is strictly their own private affair and none of the public's concern" and "Any public interference is of the nature of paternalism and tyranny, an unjustifiable infringement upon the natural liberties of free citizens," the University of Chicago economist John M. Clark argued. Moreover, he continued: "Even if one party loses in the transaction, that is his mistake, against which society has no business to protect him, and it is no one else's injury."[35] Looking back, the economist and New Deal "Brain Trust" member Benjamin Ginzburg would write, "the losses sustained by the ignorant and credulous investors" were "such a small phase of investment activity" that except for a "a routine effort at prevention through state laws, we could afford to be philosophical about the whole subject."[36]

It was the "a queer human trait" that explained why companies with "an unbroken record of earnings and dividend-payments ... frequently have difficulty in placing with investors issues bearing as high as six or seven percent," as one Wisconsin editor put it. This trait "beyond the influence of any paternal 'progressive' law" meant Blue Sky laws were failed "when it comes to 'guardianship' of the 'sucker' – who wants something for nothing – and one of whom is born every second."[37] For Theodore Roosevelt, who had once promised to sign a national Blue Sky law if elected president, it was now clear that "if either farmer, mechanic, or day laborer is shiftless or lazy, if he shirks downright hard work, if he is stupid or self-indulgent, then no law can save him."[38]Woodrow Wilson, the Progressive Democrat who defeated Roosevelt in the 1912 Presidential election, would later go still farther to declare against efforts to protect the public from folly, whether financial or otherwise, writing: "I am one of those who absolutely reject the trustee theory, the guardianship theory. ... I suspect that the people of the United States understand their own interests better than any group of men in the confines of the country understand them."[39] The fault was with the victim and not the victimizer: *caveat emptor* was the rule that rewarded the wise and the enterprising.

And so "No previous time in our history has seen such a concerted movement to break the confidence of the people in their government as an instrument for human betterment," wrote John Lapp, chairman of Marquette University's social sciences department, as he wondered

> Is the individual who loses everything in the failure of a bank or a business or a corporation thereby unfit to survive? Is the person who has been lured by a real estate broker or by the glamorous wordings of advertisements, of

booster clubs, and of chambers of commerce guilty of being unfit because he invests his all to reach El Dorado only to find the bubble has broken?[40]

Notes

1. "Wilson Addresses Club," *Topeka State Journal* March 25 1920: 6.
2. Records of the State Bank Commissioner's Office and Kansas Corporation Commission, Escrow Record (Receipts) c. 1917–1936 vol.1.
3. David Ress, "Connected Growth: Wheat and Tenant Farms in Kansas, 1880–1925," *Kansas History: A Journal of the Central Plains*, Vol. 44, No. 4 (Winter 2021–2022) 230–245.
4. Calculated from U.S. Census of 1920, Vol. 9. *Manufactures* (Washington: Census Bureau, 1923) 450, 588, 970.
5. "Unfairness, Imposition or Fraud in the Sale of Securities—So-called "Blue Sky" Law, 1915;" 1915 Kansas Session Laws at 197–98. The seven grounds were that: the offerer was insolvent or untrustworthy; the business plan was unfair, inequitable or fraudulent; the business plan did not prevent misuse of offering proceeds; that advertising material was deceptive; the stock was watered; the business itself was illegal; and that the business was a scheme to enrich promoters at the expense of investors.
6. Kansas v. Short, 247 P. 114 (Kansas Supreme Court. 1926); Harbor Business Blocks Co. v. Gregory, 169 P. 191 (Kansas Supreme Court, 1917).
7. Kansas v Bell, 193 P. 373 (Kansas Supreme Court. 1920); Lilley v. Sterling Oil & Refining Co., 197 P. 201 (Kansas Supreme Court, 1921); Weisendanger v. Lind, 220 P. 263 (Kansas Supreme Court,1923) Daniels v. Craiglow, 292 P. 771 (Kansas Supreme Court,1930).
8. "May Reorganize Securities Board," *L'Anse (Michigan) Sentinel*, January 13 1916: 3. The board was not reorganized.
9. John M. Elliot, *Annotated Blue Sky Laws of the United States* (Cincinnati: W.H. Anderson Co., 1919) 327, citing Michigan's "General Report of Securities Commission.".
10. Census of 1920, *Manufactures* 670.

11. "Law Dodged In Sale of 20 Stocks," *Omaha Sunday Bee*, August 7 1921: 1,2.
12. U.S. Census, *Manufactures*, 834.
13. "Cooperative Dollars for the Cattle Industry," *The Alliance (Nebraska) Herald*, June 12 1919: 14; "Ko-operative Dollars," *Tagliche Omaha Tribune*, June 6 1919:8; "Ko-operativni dollar" *Pokrock Zapadu*,(Omaha) July 12 1919:6; "Banks Aided Stock Fraud is Charge," *Omaha Daily Bee* July 3 1920: 1.
14. "Widow Is Called In Potash Suit," *Omaha Daily Bee*, March 4 1922: 1, 2. Four of the cattle company promoters also ran the William Berg Potash Co. offering which promised dividend payments within 90 days of the start of operations of a never-completed potash plant, for which they were eventually convicted on federal mail fraud charges—that is, for the cattle company promotion, the group found a way to dodge the federal laws. "Your stock at $100 per share has been changed to $125 and $200 on our books," one of the promoters, William H. McWhorter, wrote to one nervous victim. "There is no doubt it will soon be worth more than $200 as our plant will begin producing potash soon. You know what that will mean." "'Potash 4' May Face New Counts Next Fall, *Ibid.*, July 9 1922:9." It was letters like that that opened a path for federal prosecutors to shut down the potash promotion. Avoiding the mails, and the reluctance of small victims to come forward, left five cattle loan company promoters who had not been involved with the potash company mailings free to flee the state. They were never brought to trial. The kingpin, Ray V. McGrew, committed suicide in California seven years later. "Orders to Return Here Not Served on Cattle Loan Men," *Ibid.*, June 12 1921: 5; "Lawyer Found Dead In Office," *Imperial Valley Press* (El Centro, California) Feburary16 1928: 1.
15. "Banks Aided Stock Fraud is Charge," *Omaha Daily Bee*, July 3 1920: 1; "Cattle Loan Company Declared Bankrupt," *Ibid.*, August 18 1920: 1, 2.
16. "Two Stockselling Concerns in Morgantown Run Afoul of the State Blue Sky Law Limiting Profits,".

    Martinsburg (West Virginia) Journal, September 27 1921: 6; Beverly Rae Kimes, Henry Austin Clark Jr, *Standard catalog of American Cars. 1805–1942.(Iola, Wisconsin:* Krause Publications, 2013) 1150–1151.

17. Census of 1920, *Manufactures*, 1559.
18. "Selleck Sales Corporation," *United States Investor*, November 12 1921: 26.
19. "L.R. Steel Stock," *New York Tribune*, October 13, 1920: 16.
20. "L.R. Steel Enterprises," *United States Investor*, December 24 1921: 12; "Accomplishments of L.R. Steel," *Ibid*., August 20 1921:8-10; "Shooting Holes in the House of Steel," *Ibid*., October 25 1921:13.
21. "Eureka Croesus Mining Company" *Ibid*., July 16 1921 26.
22. "Investors Lose $36,000,000," *Seattle Star*, March 8 1923: 1 "Steel Stocks Are Being Probed," *Ibid*. January 27 1922:5; "Investment Information," *New York Tribune*, October 14, 1922: 5; "$22 million Steel Enterprises Fail," *Washington Evening Star*, March 8, 1923:2.
23. "Enormous Amount Involved in Julian Oil Stock Case," *Imperial Valley Press* (El Centro, California) June 9 1927: 1; "Oil Case Near Climax as Jury Indicts Group," *Ibid*., June 25 1927: 1.
24. "Arrest Exposes Huge Stock Swindle," *The Sunday Tulsa (Oklahoma) World*, June 4 1922: 1,19.
25. "Alleged Stock Frauds Listed in Indictments," *Washington Herald*, October 3 1922: 1,2.
26. "The Aim Of This Issue," *United States Investor*, August 6 1921: 1.
27. "Can We Curb Promoters," *Ibid*., January 28 1922: 1.
28. "Help for Ohio Investors," *Ibid*. May 13 1922: 7; "Can We Curb Promoters," *Ibid*., January 28 1922: 1; For the stepped up campaign in *United States Investor* by securities firms, see, e.g., W,W. Beal, "Uniform Blue Sky Laws Desirable," *Ibid*. October 14 1922: 30 (Beal was president of an Iowa securities dealer); Roy Osgood, "Fraudulent Security Traffic," *Ibid*., May 27 1922: 16–20 (he was vice president of a Chicago trust company).
29. "Bridge to Pay Old Investors," *Detroit Free Press*, July 6 1927: 5; "Scott is a Drug Addict, Sanity Jury is Told," August 4 1925 1, 2; "Russell T. Scott, Who Seven Times Cheated the Noose, Hangs Himself," *Regina (Saskatchewan) Leader-Post* October 10 1927:1.
30. "Western Mining Conference To Consider Problems Of High Current Importance," *The Mining Congress Journal*, May 1922: 705; "Blue-Sky Bill Critics Are In A Majority," *Ibid*., September 1922: 869.

31. "Federal Blue Sky Law Passes House But Finds Tariff Halting Progress In Senate," *Ibid*, June 1922: 1922: 748.
32. Kirby Page, Leslie Blanchard et al., *Christianity and economic problems, facts, principles, programs; a discussion group text-book*, (New York: Association Press, 1922) 36–37.
33. Otto H. Kahn, *Our economic and Other Problems; a financier's point of view* (New York: George H. Doran Co., 1920): 270–271.
34. William L. David, "What is Wrong with the Blue Sky Law?," Ohio Law Reporter, Vol. 24, (1926): 2231.
35. John M Clark, *Social Control of Business* (Chicago: University of Chicago Press, 1926): 37. He is not to be confused with his father, John Bates Clark, a pioneer of the neoclassical school of marginal analysis. John M. Clark's work focused on explaining efficiency of the huge and capital-intensive industrial corporations that were reshaping the United States economy—transforming distribution systems and product choices available even in places like Maple Hill, Kansas—even as they broadened and deepened trading on the main stock exchanges, primarily the New York Stock Exchange, through the 1920s.
36. Benjamin Ginzburg, "Wall Street Under the New Deal," *North American Review* Vol. 245 (1938): 65, 69.
37. Editorial, *The Wisconsin Tobacco Reporter* (Edgerton, Wisconsin) May 7 1915: 4.
38. Theodore Roosevelt, *Theodore Roosevelt, an autobiography* (New York: Charles Scribner's sons,1922): 160.
39. Woodrow Wilson, *The new freedom: a call for the emancipation of the generous energies of a people* (New York: Doubleday, Page, 1921): 61.
40. John A. Lapp, *Justice First* (New York: The Century Co., 1927): 176.

Bibliography

Act No, 46 "Unfairness, Imposition or Fraud in the Sale of Securities—So-called "Blue Sky" Law, 1915;" 1915 Kansas Session Laws, chapter 164

Records of the State Bank Commissioner's Office and Kansas Corporation Commission, Escrow Record (Receipts) c. 1917–1936 vol.1; Kansas State Archives, Topeka

Anonymous, 1920. "L.R. Steel Stock," *New York Tribune*, October 13: 16
———. 1921a. "Eureka Croesus Mining Company" *United States Investor*, July 16:26
———. 1921b. "The Aim Of This Issue," *United States Investor*, August 6: 1
———. 1921c. "Law Dodged In Sale of 20 Stocks," *Omaha Sunday Bee*, August 7: 1, 2
———. 1921d. "Accomplishments of L.R. Steel," *United States Investor*, August 20: 8–10
———. 1921e. "Shooting Holes in the House of Steel," *United States Investor.*, October 25:13
———. 1921f. "Selleck Sales Corporation," *United States Investor*, November 12: 26
———. 1921g. "L.R. Steel Enterprises," *United States Investor*, December 24: 12;
———. 1922a. Can We Curb Promoters," *United States Investor*, January 28: 1
———. 1922b. "Western Mining Conference to Consider Problems Of High Current Importance," *The Mining Congress Journal*, May: 705
———. 1922c. "Help for Ohio Investors," *United States Investor*. May 13: 7
———. 1922d. "Federal Blue Sky Law Passes House but Finds Tariff Halting Progress In Senate," *Ibid*, June: 748
———. 1922e. "Blue-Sky Bill Critics are in a Majority," *The Mining Congress Journal*, September: 869
———. 1922f. "Alleged Stock Frauds Listed in Indictments," *Washington Herald*, October 3: 1
———. 1923a. "Investors Lose $36,000,000," *Seattle Star*, March 8: 1
———. 1923b. "$22 million Steel Enterprises Fail," *Washington Evening Star*, March 8, 1923:2
———. 1927a. "Enormous Amount Involved in Julian Oil Stock Case," *Imperial Valley Press* (El Centro, California) June 9: 1
———. 1927b. "Bridge to Pay Old Investors," *Detroit Free Press*, July 6: 5
———. 1927c. "Russell T. Scott, Who Seven Times Cheated the Noose, Hangs Himself," *Regina (Saskatchewan) Leader-Post* October 10:1
Clark, John M. 1926. *Social Control of Business* Chicago: University of Chicago Press
Daniels v. Craiglow, 292 P. 771 (Kansas Supreme Court, 1930)
David, William L. 1926. "What is Wrong with the Blue Sky Law?," *Ohio Law Reporter*, 24: 2231
Elliot, John M. 191. *Annotated Blue Sky Laws of the United States* Cincinnati: W.H. Anderson Co.
Ginzburg, Benjamin. 1938. "Wall Street Under the New Deal," *North American Review* 245: 65-69

Kahn, Otto H. 1920. *Our Economic and Other Problems; A Financier's Point of View*. New York: George H. Doran Co.

Kansas v Bell, 193 P. 373 (Kansas Supreme Court. 1920)

Lapp John A. 1927. *Justice First* New York: The Century Co.

Lilley v. Sterling Oil & Refining Co., 197 P. 201 (Kansas Supreme Court, 1921)

Page, Kirby & Leslie Blanchard et al., 1922. *Christianity and economic problems, facts, principles, programs; a discussion group text-book*, New York: Association Press

Ress, David. 2022. "Connected Growth: Wheat and Tenant Farms in Kansas, 1880-1925," *Kansas History: A Journal of the Central Plains*, 44: 230-245

Roosevelt, Theodore. 1922. *Theodore Roosevelt, An Autobiography*. New York: Charles Scribner's Sons

Weisendanger v. Lind, 220 P. 263 (Kansas Supreme Court, 1923)

Wilson, Woodrow, 61 P. 1921. *The New Freedom: A Call for the Emancipation of the Generous Energies of a People*. New York: Doubleday

CHAPTER 9

Stock Market Expansion and the Ticker's Siren Song

Abstract Inspired by the gains many saw from selling the Liberty Loan bonds they bought to finance the U.S. military in World War I, the 1920s saw an important shift in how Americans looked at buying shares. Dividend income mattered less, as did the idea of shares represented an ownership interest to be held for a long time. Trading shares for quick profit became the goal. Stock promoters who had marketed the dubious securities the Blue Sky Acts targeted moved to "bucket shop" brokerages, investment banks sold stocks bonds their underwriters knew were trash, as the Pecora committee revealed. The stock market crash of 1929 shattered confidence in shares, but also pointed to an issue of investor protection that state law could not address.

Keywords 1929 crash · Stock exchanges · Market regulation · Investment banking

In Nampa, Idaho, W.G. Scholtz, editor of the Nonpartisan League daily newspaper, was not finding it easy to find the money to keep publishing his arguments for a party platform calling for a state-owned bank and grain elevators, like those the League had set up in North Dakota. Idaho bankers were not lending him money; dealers in grain, who were often

D. Ress, *The Kansas Blue Sky Act of 1911*,
https://doi.org/10.1007/978-3-031-43831-8_9

also operators of elevators as well as dry-goods stores and farm implement dealerships, were not enthusiastic advertisers. A paper aiming for statewide circulation was not that attractive an advertising option for the small-town merchants whose notices were the economic foundation of most local papers. To finance the paper, then, Scholtz urged farmers to exchange their safe, government-issued Liberty Loan Bonds for stock in his newspaper—and when he did, opened up a path for his opponents to attack: a charge he had violated the state's Blue Sky Act, on the grounds Scholtz's proposal netted him more money than the paper was worth.[1] The Liberty Bonds that those Idaho farmers were urged to exchange (though only the larger denominations, $50 and above, were bearer bonds and therefore transferable) were among some $17 billion-worth sold during the federal government's four Liberty Loan drives of 1917 and 1918. That enormous effort, fueled by intensive advertising and public relations campaigns appealing to American's patriotism would transform the way individuals thought about investment.

Some 20 million people bought bonds.[2] The message that buying bonds was patriotic made the Liberty Bonds' modest 3.5 to 4% annual interest payments more palatable, but the fact that the price of the bonds had jumped sharply in the weeks after the armistice ending the World War I "made millions of people conscious of the fact that money could be made by the simple process of holding paper securities until they went up in value," City College of New York economist Benjamin Ginzburg noted. And even though this belief was only half true, he added, "these millions turned to Wall Street to speculate with their surplus funds."[3]

The sales pitch that saving money by buying securities was patriotic was new; the various Mr. Thompkins of Dolley's tales had not tried that when promoting their tropical paradises. The reach of Liberty Loan campaigns was particularly broad, touching even those with modest incomes because of the installment payment plan Secretary of the Treasury William G. McAdoo devised. For those for whom a $50 bond was out of reach, as it represented the equivalent of two weeks' pay for many city residents, McAdoo's payment plan allowed people to pay as little as 25 cents each for stamps that could also pay interest. As people bought enough of these, they could then be exchanged for the tradeable bearer bonds—the bonds that Scholtz urged his readers to cash in and swap for newspaper stock.

Patriotism through investing would be a theme that the New York Stock Exchange would pick up in its 1920s campaigns to fend off the regulation that members grumbled was excessive paternalism. Owning shares, a drumbeat of stock exchange publicity emphasized, would preserve political liberty by assuring a strong national economy. On the other hand, regulation was a paternalist interference with liberty that would also undermine national strength. The post-Armistice jump in secondary market trading, meanwhile, had reaffirmed what was still the new idea for many of those small-scale savers, as Ginzburg had noted: that it was with the price movements of a stock rather than the dividend that it paid that the real gains from an investment came.

For investment bankers and stockbrokers, still grumbling about the supposed paternalism of regulation—even a suggestion that stock traders take Saturdays off in July and August prompted "indignant protests of business men who do not want paternalism in the stock market"[4]—these new notions about investment would prove a windfall. They would also allow investment bankers and stock exchanges to spin a new tale, new at least to a public that may not have been familiar with Adam Smith's rather obscure invisible hand metaphor about self-interest and the public interest. The securities firms' tale was that the most effective protection against deception and fraud was a free market through which millions bought and sold shares—a market that was growing exponentially after World War I.[5] At the same time, the securities firms' story also declared that the ordinary American was able to look after his or her own financial affairs: that archetypal independent, self-sufficient adventurer, or yeoman farmer from tales of the frontier. "Let us not belittle the small investor … proportionately, the small investor is just as wise as the man with vastly more money to invest," as New York Stock Exchange President Edward H.H. Simmons told the public.[6] The exchange's literature, and later, films, presented itself as what President Seymour L. Cromwell would deem a "people's market" for a nation of stockholders.[7] Reassured that they had the wisdom to invest prudently and—perhaps more importantly, the courage to do so—the number of Americans owning shares rose from 4.4 million in 1900 to 14.4 million in 1923 and 18 million in 1928.[8]

The nation's speculative fever was rising. It was easy to buy shares listed on a stock exchange that a state securities regulator would never see, and easy, too, for an individual to cash in for a quick profit; a telegram or phone call sufficed. It was, after all, a time when faith that American prosperity would continue forever, as Frederick Lewis Allen reported in his history of the 1920s.[9] Faith, indeed, was the word: The economist Irving Fisher said Americans put their savings into stocks on the belief they could only go higher; in a speech to a business group just days before the confidence shattered stock market crash of October 1929, he said high prices for shares were justified by companies' earnings.[10] Americans had come to believe they had found "a new and miraculous means of permanent and unlimited prosperity," the economist Virgil Jordan wrote.[11] "One day," the South Carolina restauranteur George Mehales recalled, "one of my customers showed me how much money he was making in the market. I had never even thought about the stock market before." So, "For a few days, I looked at the market page in the newspaper," he said. Then, he started buying. "The stocks I bought had gone up and up."[12]

As the 1920s boom continued, shareholders were willing to accept ever-lower dividend yields as they chased rising share prices. When, in 1918, they wanted an average annual dividend yield approaching twelve percent of the price of the shares they bought, they were still buying—and somewhat frantically—when shares offered average dividend yields of less than two percent in 1929. The decline was even sharper for mining and automobile-manufacturers' shares. Aviation shares saw a stunning drop from a yield to price ratio in 1921 almost as high as some blue promoters to barely two percent by 1929. By the middle of the decade, as radio shares began attracting significant demand, investors had grown willing to pay for shares that promised no, or virtually no, dividends.[13]

Breathless, almost daily reports about the star of the 1920s market boom, Radio Corporation of America, with sixteen or seventeen company press releases in various New York City newspapers over just one three week span in 1927, along with direct advice from columnists that it was time to buy RCA before it climbed out of reach, enticed many to "be bullish on America," as the economist Guilio Pontecorvo has noted.[14] Buyers were reassured by many a self-declared financial expert that "If a man buys a certain security because it is cheap .... he is no more playing a percentage game than if he purchases a piece of real estate because it is cheap." Speculation, in this view, was simply human nature, and if some did so foolishly "The cure lies not in paternalism, but in evolution and understanding," the Moody's stock and bond reporting service's Thomas Gibson smugly declared.[15]

Dolley felt his paternalism was justified because he believed most Kansans weren't really competent to make wise decisions about their savings, but it was not clear that some of firms rushing into the securities business in the 1920s were much better. By 1929, the firms that had dominated investment banking two decades earlier were managing barely one out of every eight stock offerings in 1929.[16] Some of those new bankers knew little more about the shares they were selling than did their customers, and their "Confessions of incompetence reached indecent proportions," as historian Michael Parrish noted. There was little other expertise available, however. Only eight states had set up specialist securities regulation agencies to enforce their Blue Sky laws, generally leaving this work to officials whose main assignment was to oversee banks' and insurance companies' solvency or handle incorporation records or general legal affairs of state government.[17] The NYSE's push to have listed companies publish financial data was minimal, and the data that was required was not particularly easy to find.[18]

At the same time, the way securities dealers reached out to potential clients was changing; in a nation where, for the first time in the 1920s, most people lived in cities, the Mr. Thompkins of the business no longer found it quite as effective to hop off a train, take a quick look at the little county weekly's obituaries, and pitch a new widow with dreams of tropical plantation riches. The pitch now was, often as not, over the telephone or in an office—for both old and new investment banks and stock brokerages were opening offices far from Wall Street, and the swindlers did, too. The boom in trading activity on the New York and regional stock markets also created a new way for con artists to play their suckers. From their so-called bucket shops, they'd take orders for well-known or much-publicized shares that they would not actually buy, for the plan was simply to take the money and run. Sometimes they'd pay their victims one or two "dividends" to hold them off for a while, sometimes they'd use the victims' funds to play the market for themselves. But just as Blue Sky laws allowed the arrest of would-be Mr. Thompkins, as Kansan officials had with R.J. Bell, and could force promoters to reimburse an investor if the deal was done in the state, as the Kansas state Supreme Court confirmed they could, they also gave state officials the tools to shut down bucket shops, as Indiana managed to, shutting down six, when New York and Massachusetts could not. "The practice of telephoning market deals must cease," Earle Coble, chief examiner for Indiana's state securities commission. "It is nefarious, in that it encourages bucket shops and fleecing would be speculators."[19]

Bucket shops were "tremendously profitable," the speculator Jesse Livermore would write. "You know how they traded in bucket shops. You gave your money to a clerk"—the margin, at the time seventy-five cents for each share for a ticket of as few as five shares—and

> When you wished to close your trade ... he took the last price or ..the next quotation „ ,and then you went to the cashier and got whatever cash it called for. Of course, when the market went against you and the price went beyond the limit set by your margin your trade automatically closed itself and your ticket became one more scrap of paper.[20]

The daily bounces in a share price were usually enough to wipe out most margins in just a few hours.

In New York, which did not have a Blue Sky law, bucket shop "producers" made a twenty-five percent commission on every sale—down from fifty percent when the shops first opened their doors. The producers' main lead was the telephone directory, especially listings for doctors, dentists, and other relatively high-income professionals or residents of high rent districts. One bucket shop took an heir to the Gardiner's Island family fortune for $68,000 with a supposed "corner" on the market for a bottling company's stock—that is, a chance to control enough of the shares to dictate to the rest of the world whatever exorbitant price the corner-maker fancied.[21] But bucket shops in states without a Blue Sky law as often as not sold the kind of mining or oil promotions that so concerned Dolley, along with the usual taking of cash for shares that the buyer never actually received. Massachusetts, also without a Blue Sky law, had to try a simple charge of larceny to convict Charles E. Brickley, star of Harvard's 1912 and1913 football teams, of the standard bucket shop scam of taking money and not delivering the stock—in his case, twenty-two shares and $2,195 from a Boston man and a smaller sum from a woman in Marlboro, Massachusetts.[22]

Years later, Americans would learn that it not only renegade Harvard footballers or con artists like Mr. Thompkins who ran stock market scams. The Senate Banking Committee hearings into the collapse of the nation's financial system led by counsel Ferdinand Pecora in 1932 revealed that even the bluest of blue-chip investment banks could be as deceptive as any glad-handing Rufus Wallingford when it came to gulling an individual with some money to spare for a flyer on the market.

There was, for instance, the tale of Edgar D. Brown, of Pottsville, Pennsylvania. He had $25,000 tucked away in U.S. Government bonds and another $75,000 when he decided to take a break from business and retire to California for his health. A magazine ad from National City Bank, suggesting it could help with the same kind of sage advice a trusted local banker offered "to keep you closely guided as regards your investments" seemed to Brown to be just the thing to make the move an easy one. When a National City salesman hastened to call on him, he nodded sagely at Brown's directive to put his cash into safe bonds. At first, that's what the salesman said he did—but he did buy the U.S. government bonds Brown probably had in mind. Instead, there were Peruvian, Chilean, Greek, and provincial German bonds, all underwritten by National City, all looking so profitable on their face—and providing no indication that some were essentially vehicles for National City to unload bad loans onto its securities affiliate's clients—that Brown was induced to borrowing money to eventually put $250,000 into these securities. National City, as it happened, had for many years before signing Brown up as a client worried about Peru's dubious credit history and political instability. Not long before its salesman convinced Mr. Brown to buy some, a bank vice president had advised the bank's president that "I have no great faith in any material betterment of Peru's economic condition." But despite the vice president's skepticism, the bank agreed to underwrite a new $15 million Peruvian bond in 1927 and followed that quickly by taking on a $50 million issue and a $25 million follow-up offering. National City sold the bonds to the public for prices ranging from $91.50 to $96.50 per $100 bond. Its spread was $5—that is, for every $91.50 it received, it passed on just $86.50 to Peru (along with a gift of $450,000 to the president's son). For the very limited capital the bank actually committed (since it collected the money first before forwarding Peru its share) its net profit of $680,000 represented a healthy return on its money. Those, like Mr. Brown, who bought the bonds, lost heavily—the bonds went into default in 1931. Anyone who wanted to bet Peru would resume interest payments could have bought a $100 face value bond for $4.625 in 1933. When Mr. Brown complained that his bonds had not performed as promised, the National City sales agent replied: "Well that it your fault for insisting upon bonds. Why don't you let me buy you some stock?"[23] So he did.

That stock turned out to be Anaconda Copper. A spike in copper prices had set National City's traders racing to acquire a large, 300,000 share block. But the spring of 1929 saw a 25% drop in copper prices and, suddenly, it seemed that those 300,000 shares represented a too-heavy commitment to a company, even when National City served as its banker and Anaconda's chairman was a National City director. To keep Anaconda shares from slumping too badly, National City bought additional shares in the open market—thereby, of course, supporting the price—but at the same time, it fed some 1.3 million Anaconda shares to its clients for $120 to $130 each in the two months before the October 1929 crash. Those were shares which had cost National City an average of $100; that is, it made a profit of twenty to thirty percent in just two months. By the time he could tell Pecora's Senate committee about his losses, Anaconda shares were trading between $7 and $10.[24]

Although Brown might not have seen things this way, and an Otto Kahn or John M. Clark surely would not have, there was very much an element of paternalism in his experience, and of willing acceptance of it. For while no state had, or could, step in between him and the broker from National City, the big bank had in fact stepped in to say, in effect: "You cannot look after your own best interests in these complex financial matters, we can act for you because we are more competent than you." For all that Brown, and millions of others, might have told themselves they were the sharp-witted business-owner, or farmer, or dealer of those particular American folk tales, they were still taken in—not just by the unfair dealing of a National City, but by the fairy tale they told themselves about who they were.

Millions of others, like the South Carolina café owner George Mehales, were taken in by something else: the siren song of the ticker. There was not really all that much else to go on. Concrete knowledge about the companies whose shares investors—rather, to be precise speculators—like Mehales bought was not particularly easy to come by. There was little help from the New York Stock Exchange's publicity-focused effort to reassure small investors. It was not until 1926 that the exchange was able to require (and enforce) a rule that all listed companies publish balance sheets and net income figures—the data, that is, that could allow investors to calculate such basic valuation ratios as share price to per share profits or assets. Barely half also published sales figures, and fewer still any information on cost of sales, which would have allowed some preliminary analysis of how well a company's management was operating the business.[25] Mehales instead tracked prices daily, though in his paper, rather than by visiting a broker's office as one Wall Street stockbroker reported his female clients would, seeking the reassurance of their paternalistic advisors. Crowding around the stock ticker, he said: "They seek more advice. They sit and murmur, 'Shall I sell or shall I hang on?' They go through greater agony of indecision in crucial moments."[26]

Mehales, who had bought a part-interest in his café with for $300 he had inherited from property in Greece along with a loan from his brother in New York, was not a particularly experienced business-owner; struggling to keep up with debts incurred for kitchen equipment, he put in long hours at the café. It was a small place, open day and night, the kind of spot that Mehales described as "a place to hang around in." In a sense, that moment when a customer's tales of stock market successes convinced him to start looking at the price quotations in the newspaper crystalized the change in mentality that swept the nation in the 1920s—and convinced him that he could understood all that was necessary to know about shares. What mattered was not what the companies themselves were doing (and in many cases they were not doing badly) but what all the other players in the market thought about the market trend, as expressed in the quotations of the daily paper. After all, they would have thought just as he did: that stocks were on the rise. Who better than the friendly fellow at the café counter to know the public mind, after all? "I had become so interested with the market that I let my own business go down," he said. "Business dropped off, but I didn't care 'cause I was making plenty of money in the market."[27]

The last week of October 1929 changed everything. At the New York Stock Exchange opening October 24, that autumn's growing sense of unease turned to panic. As sell orders flooded in share prices suddenly plunged, with the Dow Jones Industrial Average dropping by eleven percent; although a concerted buying effort by major investment banks reserved some of the decline, the selling rush resumed on Monday, as margin calls—demands on investors to put up more money on shares they had bought by only putting a small deposit down—prompted many to bail out; Dow average fell nearly thirteen percent; on Tuesday, October 29, it shed an additional nearly twelve percent. In South Carolina, the Black Thursday slump caught café-owner Mehales, who had put off making payments on loans for his restaurant fixtures, expecting his stock market profits to retire the debt. Mehales had been buying shares on margin—that is, making only a small down payment to secure a loan from his broker, just as Livermore had when he was a teenage gambler in bucket shops—but the Black Thursday slump meant he had to put down more money. "I went to the bank and put up all the cash I had in the bank with my broker. It seemed to me that things would soon get better." But the crash continued, and

> they told me I needed more cash to cover up. I couldn't get it. I was wiped out that day.... I considered killing myself, 'cause I had nothing

> left. I found out what a fool I had been. I did manage to pay my debts by selling my cafe at rock bottom prices.[28]

He and his new wife "struggled along on almost nothing;" she died in 1930. Through the hard years of the Great Depression, he kept working and eventually saved enough money to buy an interest in another small restaurant—but no more shares of stock.

Notes

1. "Wallingford Was A Great Piker," *Caldwell (Idaho) Tribune*, May 2, 1919: 8; The charge never made it to court and may have arisen from within the League before the state's Democratic Attorney General joined in. Still, it had the desired effect of neutralizing Stoltz and his paper, for the accusation "caused Idaho farmers who are members of the League to open their eyes a bit wider," especially after Scholtz expressed support for Socialist leader Eugene V Debs, "League Difficulties," Ibid., February 13, 1920: 4.
2. Richard Sutch, "Liberty Loans," Federal Reserve History, https://www.federalreservehistory.org/essays/liberty-bonds.
3. Benjamin Giznburg, "Wall Street under the New Deal," *The North American Review*, Vol. 245, No. 1 (Spring 1938): 70.
4. "Big Steel Order Boosts Market," *The Washington Herald*, June 6, 1919: 8.
5. The Invisible Hand became a much-used metaphor for the operation of a market well after Smith wrote and a reader has to look hard for it in Smith's writings, where it is not directly tied to the functioning of a market, to say nothing of a securities market. In *The Theory of Moral Sentiments*, he wrote an invisible hand would lead to nearly to same distribution of goods as if they had been divided into equal portions. Adam Smith, *The Theory of Moral Sentiments* (1758) part IV, chapter 1 paragraph 10, and in *Wealth of Nations* he wrote that the invisible hand led people seeking their own gain would benefit society more than a deliberate intent would. *An Inquiry into the Nature and Causes of the Wealth of Nations (1776)* Book IV, Chapter II, paragraph IX.
6. Edward H.H. Simmons, *Modern Capitalism and Other Addresses* (New York: New York Stock Exchange, 1927): 263.

7. Seymour L. Cromwell, *The Problems and Policies of the New York Stock Exchange* (New York: New York Stock Exchange, 1923): 5.
8. H. T. Warshow, "The Distribution of Corporate Ownership in the United States," *Quarterly Journal of Economics*, Vol. 39 (November 1924): 15–38; Gardiner Means, "The Diffusion of Stock Ownership in the United States," *Quarterly Journal of Economics*, Vol. 44 (August 1930): 561–560.
9. Frederick Lewis Allen, *Only Yesterday: An Informal History of the 1920s* (New York: Harper & Row, 1931).
10. "Fisher Sees Stocks Permanently High," *New York Times*, October 16, 1929: 8; Irving Fisher, *The Stock Market Crash and After* (New York: Macmillan, 1930): 99.
11. Virgil Jordan, "The Era of Mad Illusions," *North American Review*, Vol. 229 (1930): 55.
12. Interview of George Mehales by R.V. Williams; December 1938, U.S. Work Projects Administration, Federal Writers' Project: Folklore Project, Life Histories, 1936–1939. https://www.loc.gov/resource/wpalh3.32030213/?sp=7.
13. Dividend payments/year end share prices

	All shares (%)	*Industrials (%)*	*Mining (%)*	*Oil (%)*	*Automobiles (%)*	*Aviation (%)*	*Radio (%)*
1918	11.9	13.6	14.3	7.1	24.6	n.a.	n.a.
1919	8.1	7.1	6.7	4.1	10.0	n.a.	n.a.
1920	9.5	8.4	9.9	4.4	10.3	n.a.	n.a.
1921	11.8	11.3	12.2	9.0	28.8	43.3	n.a.
1922	8.6	8.3	5.4	8.9	15.2	34.9	n.a.
1923	8.6	8.1	9.5	5.2	18.2	27.5	n.a.
1924	8.1	7.5	15.0	4.5	18.0	18.5	0
1925	5.8	5.4	7.3	3.7	11.8	4.5	0
1926	5.3	5.2	4.2	4.3	7.9	2.1	0.4
1927	4.0	4.0	3.0	4.3	4.2	0.9	2.3
1928	2.7	2.5	2.0	3.3	1.8	0.1	0.4
1929	1.8	1.9	0.9	2.5	2.1	0.04	0.2

Source Calculated from **The Cowles Commission for Research in Economics data; Average dividends** at https://view.officeapps.live.com/op/view.aspx?src=https%3A%2F%2Fsom.yale.edu%2Fsites%2Fdefault%2Ffiles%2F2021-12%2FYields-Cowles.xls&wdOrigin=BROWSELINK, average share prices at https://view.officeapps.live.com/op/view.aspx?src=https%3A%2F%2Fsom.yale.edu%2Fsites%2Fdefault%2Ffiles%2F2021-12%2FStock_Price-Annavg-1871-1940-Cowles.xls&wdOrigin=BROWSELINK

14. Guilio Pontecorvo, "Investment Banking and Security Speculation in the Late 1920's," *The Business History Review*, Vol. 32, No. 2 (Summer 1958): 183.
15. Thomas Gibson, *The Cycles of Speculation* (New York: Moody Magazine and Book Co., 1917): 12–13.
16. Paul Mahoney, "The Political Economy of the Securities Act of 1933," *Journal of Legal Studies,* Vol. 30 (2001): 13.
17. Michael Parrish, *Securities Regulation and the New Deal* (New Haven: Yale University Press, 1970): 33. 34; "Securities Regulation and the New Deal," PhD thesis, Yale University, 1968: 28.
18. Mary O'Sullivan, "The Expansion of the U.S. Stock Market, 1885—1930: Historical Facts and Theoretical Fashions," *Enterprise & Society*, Vol. 8, No. 3 (September 2007): 529–530.
19. "Bucket Shops Closed," *The Indianapolis Times*, May 20, 1929: 1.
20. Edwin Lefèvre (Jesse Livermore), *Reminiscences of a Stock Operator* (New York: Wiley, 2006 [1923]): 4.6.
21. "Bucketing Salesmen Learn Selling Talks and Tricks in 'School'," and "9 Indicted in Bucketing," *New York Herald*, February, 1922: 1, 6, 7.
22. "Brickley Guilty Is Jury's Report," *New Britain (Connecticut) Herald*, March 1, 1928: 1.
23. Ferdinand Pecora, *Wall Street Under Oath* (New York: Simon & Schuster 1939): 84–86, 94–95.
24. Ibid., 86, 101–102.
25. O'Sullivan, "The Expansion of the U.S. Stock Market," 529–530.
26. "Women Gamblers Quit Wall Street," *Washington (D.C.) Evening Star*, October 30, 1929: 5.
27. Interview of George Mehales by R.V. Williams; December 1938, U.S. Work Projects Administration, Federal Writers' Project: Folklore Project, Life Histories, 1936–1939. https://www.loc.gov/resource/wpalh3.32030213/?sp=7.
28. Ibid.

Bibliography

Allen, Frederick Lewis. 1931. *Only Yesterday: An Informal History of the 1920s.* New York: Harper & Row.

Anonymous. 1918. "Wallingford Was A Great Piker," *Caldwell (Idaho) Tribune*, May 2: 8.

———. 1922. "Bucketing Salesmen Learn Selling Talks and Tricks in 'School'," and "9 Indicted in Bucketing," *New York Herald*, February 16: 1, 6, 7.

———. 1929a. "Bucket Shops Closed," *The Indianapolis Times*, May 20: 1.

———. 1929b. "Fisher Sees Stocks Permanently High," *New York Times*, October 16: 8.

———. 1929c. "Women Gamblers Quit Wall Street," *Washington (D.C.) Evening Star*, October 30, 1929: 5.

Cromwell, Seymour L. 1923. *The Problems and Policies of the New York Stock Exchange* New York: New York Stock Exchange.

Ginzburg, Benjamin. 1938. "Wall Street under the New Deal," *The North American Review*, 245: 65–70.

Mahoney, Paul. 2001. "The Political Economy of the Securities Act of 1933," *Journal of Legal Studies*, 30: 1–31.

Means, Gardiner. 1930. "The Diffusion of Stock Ownership in the United States," *Quarterly Journal of Economics*, 44: 561–560.

Interview of George Mehales by R.V. Williams. 1938, U.S. Work Projects Administration, Federal Writers' Project: Folklore Project, Life Histories, 1936–1939.

O'Sullivan, Mary. 2007. "The Expansion of the U.S. Stock Market, 1885—1930: Historical Facts and Theoretical Fashions," *Enterprise & Society*, 8, no 3 (September 2007); 489–542.

Parrish, Michael. 1970. *Securities Regulation and the New Deal*. New Haven: Yale University Press.

———. 1968. "Securities Regulation and the New Deal," PhD thesis, Yale University.

Ferdinand Pecora, Ferdinand. 1939. *Wall Street Under Oath*. New York: Simon & Schuster.

Pontecorvo, Guilio. "Investment Banking and Security Speculation in the Late 1920's," *The Business History Review*, 32: 166–191.

Simmons, Edward H.H. 1927. *Modern Capitalism and Other Addresses*. New York: New York Stock Exchange.

Warshow, H.T. "The Distribution of Corporate Ownership in the United States," *Quarterly Journal of Economics*, 39: 15–38.

CHAPTER 10

Paternalism and Liberty in the Market: Not quite a Naïf, Not quite a Con Man

Abstract The New Deal's securities regulation did not follow Dolley's Kansas Blue Sky model, despite Franklin Roosevelt's early hints that it might. Ultimately, the Blue Sky Act reflected a vanished view of investment and of neighborly buying and selling in small, self-contained economies, such as the one Kansas Banking Commissioner Joseph N. Dolley had operated in as a credit-granting grocer and banker. Ultimately, too, the initial acceptance and later rejection of the Kansas model reflects a shift in American attitudes about the opposition of paternalism and liberty.

Keywords Securities Act of 1933 · Blue Sky law · Investor protection · Mutual funds

During the 1932 presidential campaign, Franklin Roosevelt reminded graduating students at Oglethorpe University that when they started their studies before the Crash of 1929 they probably noticed that many people, "once they had accumulated a few dollars" read a tale "the hieroglyphics called stock quotations" told and decided "that their wealth was mounting miraculously without any work or effort on their part." At other times on the campaign trail, Roosevelt told the tale of an unnamed, probably fictional, upstate New York village of 125 families where 109

D. Ress, *The Kansas Blue Sky Act of 1911*,
https://doi.org/10.1007/978-3-031-43831-8_10

lost all their savings in the stock market. "I believe in the sacredness of private property," he said, but "I do not believe it should be subjected to the ruthless manipulation of professional gamblers in the stock markets." To stop them, if elected, he promised federal oversight of trading, better disclosure of corporations' financial position and that he would make "every effort to prevent the issue of manufactured and unnecessary securities … which are brought out merely for the purposed of enriching those handle their sale." Disclosure was sovereign remedy investment bankers had proposed; blocking unnecessary securities was exactly what Kansas model Blue Sky Acts aimed at.[1] Initial drafts of the legislation that would become the Securities Act of 1933 that would have empowered regulators to revoke an offering could not get past a House committee, and the securities lawyers and law professors the White House summoned to fix the problem summarily rejected any kind of merit review, dismissing what New Deal Brain Truster Benjamin Ginzburg called "the more or less ineffective policing that used to be furnished by state 'blue sky' laws."[2]

Making the case for the Blue Sky Act, Kansas Bank Commissioner Joseph N. Dolley's tales told Americans they were naïve innocents whose savings needed to be protected by people, like himself, who knew more about business than they did. Despite the grumblings of investment bankers Warren Hayden or Otto Kahn about paternalism and a threat to liberty, there was much appeal in the notion of a wise man to look out for you. Dolley's unspoken twin messages were of most Kansans' incompetence in money matters (excepting, of course, men like himself) and of the unsuitability of most shares as vehicles for Kansans' savings. These messages might have seemed an easy target for attack on grounds of a paternalistic overreach of government power, but they in fact had a strong appeal. Even now, with federal regulatory approach that aims at ensuring sufficient information is available to allow investors to make informed decisions about where to put their money, many people happily surrender the nerve-wracking work of placing their bets to others: the managers of mutual funds, or the soothingly assurances of their brokers or financial advisors standing in (not-quite) loco parentis.

Perhaps it should be no surprise that fund sales boomed after World War II, at a time when U.S. Securities Act of 1933 could allow would-be automaker Kaiser-Frazer Corp. to sell some $36 million worth of shares simply by filing a prospectus with the U.S. Securities and Exchange Commission. The firm knew better than to try in its home state after Michigan state Corporations and Securities Commissioner Howard W.

Warner told the company that selling stock at a price that was more than twenty times earnings per share and well above 200% of book value would not meet the Michigan Blue Sky law standards of fairness to investors.[3] Ohio and North Carolina also barred sales of the issue. In the end, people who fell for the unlikely dream that an undercapitalized newcomer could compete against the Big Three automakers lost heavily as the shares quickly fell to half their value—and kept dropping. Securities and Exchange Commission chairman Donald Cook might complain that his agency had been left in the dark about Kaiser-Frazer's finances, but the price-earnings ratio and book value tests Warner used to weigh the fairness of the offering or the even simpler look at the company's lack of profits that prompted Ohio Commissioner Ernest Cornell's ban were easy enough to see, if the question of whether an offering was appropriate had been the SEC's focus.[4] State Blue Sky laws providing for merit review barred stocks that, if not fraudulent were simply masking corporate incompetence and so were simply inappropriate for sale to the public; the SEC could not—as cases as recent as the failures of Enron, Tyco and WorldCom suggest.

The tales Dolley and opponents of the Blue Sky laws told also link the story of capital markets regulation to deeper currents of social and cultural change, the intangible evolution of mentalities, and the inner world of thought and feeling. These tales tell of paternalism versus liberty; of the stability of being part of a community of neighbors versus the thrill being involved in a nation on the move; of trusting others versus trusting oneself. By stepping along the mid-continent Main Streets where the political impetus for Blue Sky laws emerged, and where the 1920s boom would prove so seductive, this story of regulation and liberty is not so much a story of Wall Street as it is a tale of a once-upon-a-time place like Maple Hill. It is a story about what happened to these places of memory and myth as a national (and eventually international) economy grew and flourished.

So Joseph N. Dolley was easily cast in the role of that annoying but indispensable figure—the Kansas banker of folklore, half wise counselor, half busybody. In Maple Hill, Dolley had extended store credit, made loans, offered investment advice, bought stakes in neighbors' businesses. Still, when those neighbors thought Dolley, as Speaker of the Kansas House of Representatives, got a bit too high and mighty for a Maple Hill man, they stunned the rest of the state by refusing to re-elect him.[5]

Shortly afterward, Dolley would be twitted at Topeka's Saturday Night Club of lawyers and bankers with a song:

> Goodbye Dolley, you must leave us, though it breaks your heart to go
> Something in the woods is calling, and it calls for Joe,"

followed by a skit in which a bank robber sold the "commissioner" a million dollars' worth of "Black Bass Muzzle Co." Irritated, and trying not to show it too obviously, Dolley snapped back with the sour comment that when a blue sky merchant came to town, his first stop was to first seek the banker's endorsement and then a lawyer's.[6]

If Dolley was the Kansas banker of folklore, he was also formally part of the Progressive movement, "one of the field generals of Kansas insurgency," as a Kansas City editor put it, although many progressives considered him too willing to compromise with Republican stand-patters.[7] Yet the Kansas Blue Sky Act was not an part of the Kansas Progressive Republican platform, it was not supported by many progressives; it was rooted in the values of isolated, self-contained communities, as in rural Kansas, not in Progressive Era ideology that some scholars see as the source of Blue Sky laws.[8] In places like Dolley's Maple Hill, the way people thought about owning a share in a company meant either intimate, direct involvement in running the enterprise, as was the case with, for instance, the Bargain Store or as a kind of savings account that would yield a regular return—the idea that savings equals investment, a convention of economic theory, does not reflect the way that Dolley or his Maple Hill neighbors actually thought.

For the way rural Kansans (and other rural people and Americans nostalgic for that rurality) thought about investing, about caveat emptor and allowing a high-handed Main Street grandee character make decisions for them, rather than the way economists now explain the generation of capital is important in explaining the Blue Sky law movement. The Blue Sky Act was the personal crusade of just that sort of rural Kansan and it was popular with just that sort of person. It arose from Dolley's personal experience, things he heard, situations he wished he could have fixed from his desk at the Stockgrowers State Bank in Maple Hill. Its genesis was not a lawyer's analysis of a flaw in *caveat emptor*, nor an economist's suggestion for a way to resolve a market failure, but rather simply the decision to use his office as Bank Commissioner to provide the same kind of advice he had tried to offer to his neighbors in Wabaunsee County. His electoral failure in 1910 surely reminded him that the folkways of places like Maple Hill were where his political prospects were rooted: the Blue Sky Act soon followed.

The conviction of the busybody that he or she knows better than most others was not, in Joseph Dolley, limited to the sphere of stock investment: his initiative was not so much a product of cool analysis but rather an extension of his view of himself as the wise counselor to his more naïve neighbors, a self-image so easily confirmed in tales of wise elders and their sage counsel. It was when acting in precisely this folk-tale role of guardian of less able neighbors, rather than from a view of what best served bankers like himself, that Dolley had moved to cap bank interest rates, to set minimum net worth standards for banks' stockholders, and to require a bank-financed fund to reimburse depositors when banks failed, like his views about oil and mining share promotions and when a business's financial position was secure enough for it to earn the right to sell stock and bonds to the public, reflected a comprehensive vision of the way financial affairs ought to be conducted. He was a typical small-town banker in his beliefs about finance but he was no tool of small-town bankers worried about losing business to Wall Street, as some scholars suggest; at one point he threatened to sell the homes of failed banks' directors and convict them of crimes to ensure that depositors were made whole.[9] Dolley's was a vision of finance and commerce that was fundamentally about what one neighbor owed another—even if the one was a wealthy banker and the other a humble farmworker—anchored in the well-ordered world of the miniature economy of a Kansan farm town.

From advising people about unsuitable investments—offers that they were unable to evaluate for themselves—to simply barring such offers altogether was not, to Dolley, a natural extension of a function he had long carried out as the central, organizing actor of a miniature economy's financial interactions. To step beyond giving advice to act more directly, like Kansan saloon-wrecker and temperance crusader Carrie Nation, by banning some sales is more like what busybody attempts than a mere banker dares. To simply ban a product because a measurable part of the public did not know enough about to avoid a foolish decision to buy it was an innovation in protection of the public that was out of step with the consensus of jurisprudence—that is, the *caveat emptor* rule—and with other Progressive Era initiatives. It came from time before caveat emptor, from places where caveat emptor and miniature community folkways governed the way individuals dealt with one another. It assumed something that seemed obvious enough to the writers of Justinian's code and in the civil law systems that evolved from it, but dangerous for a political actor in a democratic society: that there were times when individuals were too incapable of looking out for themselves. The Blue Sky Act effectively said they were.

Incompetence is why the state justifies its interventions care for people with mental illness or intellectual disabilities; it is why children are not allowed to vote or drive. Incompetence, once declared, necessarily results in a constraint of choice and sometimes, if not always on liberty: the doors of psychiatric wards and Alzheimer's wards in nursing homes are locked. The Investment Bankers Association formed largely in response to Dolley's campaign focused their attack on the implication of incompetence: the answer, they argued, was disclosure.

The public, once informed of the financial status and plans of a business seeking funds, was wise enough to look out for itself, the investment bankers argued. They said the interjection of the state between buyer and seller and the substitution of an official's judgment for the potential buyer's was an infringement of liberty, when Dolley believed it was really about what was safe to choose. The association did not accept Dolley's small-town view that some deals just should not be done, such as buying stock in start-up businesses based on unproven technology or claims on natural resources when the promoters had not put in their own money. Failure in business, in life or in investing was simply price of progress, for most business executives, economists, and politicians, and their argument that regulation was paternalism was easier to accept when the market boom of the 1920s made failure by betting wrong on the next tick of a stock price seem remote.

"It is impossible in the very nature of things for bureaucracy to go together with efficiency in a democracy," as Kuhn Loeb partner Otto Kahn argued, adding: "Nor, indeed, can paternalism and liberty exist side by side."[10] Using law or even charity for "protections of the individual against his own weakness" simply would "make defective quality … as entitled to existence as strength," Tennessee iron works owner Henry Sanford wrote. "Our emotionalists dote on paternalism … The majority of those sentimental idealists who support such views have never reckoned on the fundamental reality of life, or on its largest problem." That problem, in his view, was the evolutionary one of survival of the fittest.[11]

Liberty, in the view of an Otto Kahn, a Sanford or the Investment Bankers Association's leaders, when extended to financial dealings militated against any outsider's effort to get between buyer and seller. Yet, in a sense, the public voted with its money to accept exactly that. From 1940, when the Investment Company Act authorized federal oversight of mutual funds, through the stagnant 1940s, Americans put billions of dollars into mutual funds—that is in the hands of others who believed, as Dolley had, that they were more expert than most when it came to evaluating investments. Mutual fund net assets grew by nearly five times—462%—by 1950. Even through the long bull market of the 1980s and 1990s, individuals still opted to let others manage their savings: mutual fund net assets increased 20-fold over those decades.[12]

Convinced of an opposition of liberty and legislation, these enemies of the paternalism they saw embodied in Blue Sky law, shrugged off the point that liberty (as the legal historian James Willard Hurst wrote) is "the enlargement of options ... created by laws which secure public health, education, the market and peaceable political processes."[13] When Dolley's way of protecting the public finally came before the Supreme Court, the high court decided that the Constitution's guarantee of liberty did not include the freedom to lure others to make an improvident decisions and so take their property; the state's obligation to protect its people should not be compromised "upon the assertion of an absolute liberty of conduct which does not exist," the court ruled.[14]

Freedom and constraint, then, is a balancing act. Tales told about what liberty entails, what paternalism supposedly is, are the framework within which the balance is struck. So Dolley could comfortably say he did not mind when critics complained of the law's paternalism, for he had tales that resonated strongly—at least, back home in Kansas. "It has been said that the people do not need a guardian to supervise their investments. Why not?" Dolley said:

> Why should the bank be regulated and supervised any more so than the stock selling company? History and statistics show that losses through banks are but a drop in the bucket compared with the money which is lost through investment in worthless stocks and bonds.[15]

Feeling helpless when hearing tales of the various Mr. Thompkins plaguing the countryside, the financial publisher John Moody grumbled that "There is an old saying that the American public likes to be fooled

… it would seem that the saying has lost none of its truthfulness."[16] In the end, the story of Blue Sky and Buyer Beware is tale about tales, tales of get rich quick schemes, about paternalism, about liberty, about small-town virtues, and the nature of investment. When a Dodge City grocer or book-keeper puts money into the Bargain Store, when a Joseph Dolley backed a Maple Hill blacksmith so he could open his workshop, they were doing something fundamentally different than George Mehales's speculation in the stock market. The one was a creative act; the other, a fiction told Americans a sure path to wealth. Dolley once had declared that newspaper stories about a Wall Street slump should not worry Kansans since "the American people have been fleeced long enough and have decided to quit an unequal game," and they now had a Blue Sky Act to even the playing field.[17] Even the busybody and wise counselor, it seems, might be fooled—or fool himself.

Notes

1. Oglethorpe University Commencement Address (speech file 476), May 22, 1932; Columbus, Ohio—Campaign Speech (speech file 490), August 20, 1932, Franklin D. Roosevelt, Master Speech File, 1898–1945, Franklin D. Roosevelt Presidential Library & Museum; Michael Parrish, "Securities Regulation and the New Deal," PhD dissertation, Yale University, 1968: 47.
2. Benjamin Ginzburg, "Wall Street Under the New Deal," *North American Review*, Vol. 245 (1938): 69.
3. "Stock Barred in Michigan Sells," *The Ypsilanti (Michigan) Daily Press,* January 29, 1946: 4. Warner's opinion here was not unreasonable. On the secondary market for already-issued shares of stock, buyers and sellers pretty much accepted that guideline for the next forty-five years, except for two brief spikes in the average price-to-earnings for companies in the Standard & Poors 500 index in shares in 1946 and 1962, see S and P 500 PE Ratio 90 Year Historical Chart. https://www.macrotrends.net/2577/sp-500-pe-ratio-price-to-earnings-chart. The offering would not be enough.
4. Study of the Securities and Exchange Commission, Eighty-second Congress: Final report of the Securities and Exchange Commission Subcommittee to the Committee on Interstate and Foreign Commerce (Washington: Government Printing Office, 1952): 55, 59 "Ohio Threatens to Bar New York Curb from Trading in the State," *Evening Star* (Washington, DC), June 17, 1946: 14.

5. "Seen from the Gallery," *Topeka Daily State Journal*, January 12, 1911: 9.
6. "Not A Cog Slips," Ibid., May 15, 1911: 7.
7. "Politics a Bore," *Kansas City Journal*, November 16, 1910: 1.
8. See, e.g., Vincent Carosso, Investment Banking in America (Cambridge: Harvard University Press, 1970); Rick A. Fleming, "100 Years of Securities Law: Examining a Foundation Laid in the Kansas Blue Sky," Washburn Law Journal, Vol. 50, no. 3 (Spring 2011): 583–610 and Edward J. Balleisen, *Fraud. An American History from Barnum to Madoff* (Princeton: Princeton University Press, 2017).
9. Jonathan R. Macey & Geoffrey P. Miller, "Origin of the Blue Sky Laws," *Texas Law Review*, Vol. 70 (1991): 348–397; Paul.G. Mahoney, "The Origins of the Blue-Sky Laws: A Test of Competing Hypotheses," *The Journal of Law & Economics*, Vol. 46, No. 1 (April 2003): 229–225. Dolley's threat is found "Not A Cent of Cash," *Topeka State Journal*, February 25, 1910: 1.
10. Otto Kahn, "A Real 'War' After The War," *Evening Public Ledger* (Philadelphia), September 27, 1918: 14.
11. Hugh W. Sanford, *The Business of Life*, Vol. 2 (New York: Oxford University Press, 1924), 831.
12. Mutual fund net assets:

	Net assets
	(millions)
1940	$ 450
1945	$ 1,280
1950	$ 2,530
195	$ 7,840
1960	$ 17,030
1965	$ 35,220
1970	$ 47,620
1975	$ 45,87
1980	$ 134,760
1985	$ 495,390
1990	$ 1,064,340
199	$ 2,807,610
2000.	$ 6,969,000

Source Investment Company Institute 2021 fact book, Data Section, Table 1. https://view.officeapps.live.com/op/view.aspx?src=https%3A%2F%2Fwww.icifactbook.org%2Fxls%2F21_fb_table1.xls&wdOrigin=BROWSELINK

13. James Willard Hurst, *Law and the Conditions of Freedom in the Nineteenth Century United States* (Madison: University of Wisconsin Press, 1956): 37.
14. Hall v. Geiger-Jones Co., 242 U.S. 539 (U.S. Supreme Court, 1917 at 554–555.
15. "The Kansas 'Blue Sky Law," *Central Law Journal*, September 20, 1912: 222.
16. John Moody, *The Art of Wall Street Investing* (New York: The Moody Corp., 1906): 111.
17. "Hey-Dey of Wall Street Waning?" *Topeka Daily Capital*, April 12, 1911: 1.

Bibliography

Anonymous. 1910. "Politics a Bore," *Kansas City Journal*, November 16: 1.

———. 1911a. "Seen from the Gallery," *Topeka Daily State Journal*, January 12: 9.

———. 1911b. "Hey-Dey of Wall Street Waning?" *Topeka Daily Capital*, April 12 1911: 1.

———. 1911c. "Not A Cog Slips," Ibid., May 15: 7.

———. 1912. "The Kansas 'Blue Sky Law'," *Central Law Journal*, September 20 1912: 222.

———. 1946. "Stock Barred in Michigan Sells," *The Ypsilanti (Michigan) Daily Press*, January 29: 4.

———. 1946. "Ohio Threatens to Bar New York Curb from Trading in the State," *Evening Star* (Washington, DC), June 17: 14.

Carosso, Vincent. 1970. *Investment Banking in America*. Cambridge: Harvard University Press.

Fleming, Rick. 2011. "100 Years of Securities Law: Examining a Foundation Laid in the Kansas Blue Sky," *Washburn Law Journal*, 50: 583–610.

Ginzburg, Benjamin. 1938. "Wall Street Under the New Deal," *North American Review* 245: 65–70.

Hall v. Geiger-Jones Co., 242 U.S. 539 (U.S. Supreme Court, 1917) at 554–555.

Hurst, James Willard. 1956. *Law and the Conditions of Freedom in the Nineteenth Century United States* Madison: University of Wisconsin Press.

Kahn, Otto. 1918. "A Real 'War' After The War," *Evening Public Ledger* (Philadelphia), September 27: 14.

Macey, Jonathan & Geoffrey P. Miller. 1991. "Origin of the Blue Sky Laws," *Texas Law Review* 70: 348–397.

Mahoney, Paul G. "The Origins of the Blue-Sky Laws: A Test of Competing Hypotheses," *The Journal of Law & Economics*, 46: 229–225.

Moody, John. 1906. *The Art of Wall Street Investing*. New York: The Moody Corp.

Parrish, Michael. 1968. "Securities Regulation and the New Deal," PhD dissertation, Yale University.

Roosevelt, Franklin. 1932a. Oglethorpe University Commencement Address (speech file 476), May 22, 1932 Franklin D. Roosevelt, Master Speech File, 1898–1945, Franklin D. Roosevelt Presidential Library & Museum.

———. 1932b. Columbus, Ohio—Campaign Speech (speech file 490), August 20, 1932, Ibid.

Sanford, Hugh W. 1924. *The Business of Life*. New York: Oxford University Press.

U.S. Congress. 1952. *Study of the Securities and Exchange Commission, Eighty-second Congress: Final report of the Securities and Exchange Commission Subcommittee to the Committee on Interstate and Foreign Commerce*. Washington: Government Printing Office.

Index

D. Ress, *The Kansas Blue Sky Act of 1911*,
https://doi.org/10.1007/978-3-031-43831-8

SPRINGER NATURE

GPSR Compliance

The European Union's (EU) General Product Safety Regulation (GPSR) is a set of rules that requires consumer products to be safe and our obligations to ensure this.

If you have any concerns about our products, you can contact us on ProductSafety@springernature.com

In case Publisher is established outside the EU, the EU authorized representative is:

Springer Nature Customer Service Center GmbH
Europaplatz 3
69115 Heidelberg, Germany